THE DEFEAT OF THE MIND

EUROPEAN PERSPECTIVES

EUROPEAN PERSPECTIVES

A Series in Social Thought and Cultural Criticism

Lawrence D. Kritzman, Editor

European Perspectives presents English translations of
books by leading European thinkers. With both classic
and outstanding contemporary works, the series aims to
shape the major intellectual controversies of our day and
to facilitate the tasks of historical understanding.

THE DEFEAT OF THE MIND

ALAIN FINKIELKRAUT

translation and introduction by
JUDITH FRIEDLANDER

NEW YORK   COLUMBIA UNIVERSITY PRESS

Columbia University Press
New York   Chichester, West Sussex

La Défaite de la pensée copyright © 1987 Éditions Gallimard
Copyright © 1995 Columbia University Press
All rights reserved

Library of Congress Cataloging-in-Publication Data
Finkielkraut, Alain.
[Défaite de la pensée.   English]
The defeat of the mind / Alain Finkielkraut ;
translation and introduction by Judith Friedlander.
p.   cm. — (European perspectives)
ISBN 0-231-08022-0
1. Civilization, Modern—1950-
2. Civilization, Modern—Philosophy. 3. Culture.
I. Title.   II. Series.
CB428.F5612   1995
909. 8'01—dc20   94-34464
                                              CIP

Printed in the United States of America
c 10 9 8 7 6 5 4 3 2 1

to Elisabeth

to Béatrice

CONTENTS

> *I think that in no country in the civilized world is less attention paid to philosophy than in the United States. The Americans have no philosophical school of their own, and they care but little for all the schools into which Europe is divided, the very names of which are scarcely known to them.*
>
> —*ALEXIS DE TOCQUEVILLE*

As I read *The Defeat of the Mind*, I thought of what Tocqueville observed more than 150 years ago. We might defend the erudition and vision of our Founding Fathers, but from Tocqueville's point of view, Americans were not interested in philosophy. Compared to the French and the Germans, we did not, and still do not have, a deep philosophical tradition. And the absence of one has weakened our intellectual life in many ways, most recently in the flood of articles and books concerned with the "culture wars." Scholars and journalists have written prolifically about multiculturalism, nationalism, and democracy in the modern world, but they rarely make arguments in philosophical terms, or consider debates taking place today in relation to those that raged in Europe during the eighteenth and nineteenth centuries, when French and German schools of philosophy vigorously discussed whether one could reconcile the universalistic ideals of democratic theory with the powerful pull of ethnic nationalism. Alain Finkielkraut's book places the current controversy in philosophical and historical perspective.

Obviously it would be wrong to claim that Americans still have no schools of philosophy or that intellectuals here continue to ignore debates taking place in Europe. But with few exceptions those writing about poststructuralism, for example, or sexuality and power, are more likely to be literary, cultural, or feminist critics than philosophers. This should hardly be cause for alarm, some might say, rather confirmation of the fact that the dominant Anglo-American school of analytic philosophy has failed to attract students interested in these matters. Since the 1950s those eager to study questions of concern to continental thinkers have preferred in many cases to abandon philosophy rather than identify with the discipline, defined as it was in the majority of American universities. Nevertheless, even if we sympathize with the choice many intellectuals have made, there is still a problem, for Americans committed to "doing French theory" do not, for the most part, have much of a background in the philosophical literature that informs the works of, say, Derrida and Foucault.

Despite Finkielkraut's concerns, France maintains a strong philosophical tradition. While things are changing, serious students bound for university still take courses in philosophy as a regular part of their high school curriculum, no matter what they plan to specialize in later. Before turning to Derrida and Foucault, who are rarely read in French philosophy classes either, students have gained at least some familiarity with the major figures of the Enlightenment, with the German Romantics, with Hegel and Marx. In all likelihood they have also read some ancient and medieval philosophy and studied Latin or Greek.

Alain Finkielkraut is a product of the French educational system. Born in the late 1940s and raised in Paris, he attended some of the best schools in the country. After passing his high school baccalaureate exam, he spent two years in a university preparatory program (hypokhâgne and khâgne) at the prestigious Lycée Henri IV. There he studied for and passed the highly competitive exam that earned him entrance to the Ecole Normale Supérieure de Saint Cloud, one of the *grandes écoles* where generations of French intellectuals have been trained. Although Finkielkraut majored in literature, he continued, like many of his fellow students, to study philosophy as well.

Today Alain Finkielkraut is one of France's leading public intellectuals. He is the author of many books that deal with the nation and nationalism, identity politics, particularly Jewish identity politics, the Holocaust, and historical revisionism. He has also written on the works of Charles Péguy and Emmanuel Lévinas. At the present time he is finishing a book on Hannah Arendt. Finkielkraut also edits the journal *Le Messager européen* and has a radio talk show, "Le Divan," where he brings intellectuals and public figures together to discuss pressing political and cultural issues.[1]

The son of Polish Jewish immigrants, Finkielkraut came of age in the 1960s. Like other intellectuals of his generation, he identified with the left and participated actively in the student movement that led to the uprising in 1968. But Finkielkraut broke with the student left in the early 1970s around issues of nationalism and racism, in response to the way some of his comrades had turned their critique of Israel into a more generalized attack against Jews. A few of these *gauchistes* even went so far as to support right-wing revisionists in their efforts to "prove" that the Holocaust never happened. Still, Finkielkraut remained committed to the ideals of socialism, and he joined the Cercle Gaston Crémieux, a group inspired by the Yiddish-speaking Jewish Bund of Eastern Europe, which opposed the hegemony of French culture and the nation-state. Founded in the late 1960s, the Cercle Gaston Crémieux led young intellectuals to think philosophically, historically, and strategically about what it meant to challenge the French model of "one nation within one state" and create the conditions necessary for ethnic pluralism to flourish. The cercle sought ways of establishing a secular Jewish tradition in France, which could develop, it hoped, alongside a whole range of other national minority cultures. Its reflection and activities influenced others to form groups to combat racism (SOS-Racisme) and promote minority cultures (Le Droit à la différence).

Finkielkraut, however, soon abandoned minority nationalism as well and embraced the assimilationist ideals long associated with the French nation-state. He made his way back to this classical position through the work of the philosopher Emmanuel Lévinas, a man of Lithuanian Jewish origins who came to France in the 1920s to study at the University of Strasbourg. Drawing on German phenomenology and the Russian Jewish Enlightenment, Lévinas has written extensively on the problem of confronting the other, whom he describes and analyzes as a discrete individual in the true Enlightenment tradition. Following his mentor, Finkielkraut makes a strong case in *The Defeat of the Mind* for supporting the model of the French democratic nation, arguing that the rights of the other as an individual come before the collective rights of the other's ethnic group.

Finkielkraut contrasts the French Enlightenment model of the contract-nation—where the individual chooses freely to become a citizen—with the German model of the *Volk*, where the individual can only join the nation if he or she belongs to the ethnic group. Refusing to reduce people to their cultural origins, Finkielkraut describes how the French were not always faithful to the principles of the French Enlightenment or the Germans to the German Romantic movement. Some of the best parts of his book recount critical moments in history when influential French and German intellectuals changed philosophical sides. Finkielkraut recalls, for example, how immediately after the Franco-Prussian War, and then again during the Dreyfus affair, powerful factions in France embraced the German romantic idea of the *Volksgeist* while remaining vehemently anti-German. He also draws a beautiful portrait of Goethe, who remained true to the French Enlightenment ideal of a universal culture at a time when the Germans were suffering a humiliating defeat at the hands of Napoleon.

In his discussion of Herder Finkielkraut focuses more on the uses made of the German philosopher's ideas than he does on the philosopher himself. He is particularly concerned about the way ethnic-race nationalists of the nineteenth and twentieth centuries have manipulated the *Volksgeist,* allowing it to justify, eventually, the horrors of the Final Solution and "ethnic cleansing." He also worries about the seemingly more benign application of the concept by social scientists and third world intellectuals who have infused their campaigns for cultural diversity with the romantic—and European—spirit of the *Volksgeist.*

During the nineteenth century, Finkielkraut observes, philosophers receded from the debate and social scientists took their place, in particular anthropologists, who have continued to play an important role to the present day. Finkielkraut gives the example of Lévi-Strauss, who made a forceful critique of the Enlightenment in the years following World War II. Presenting his argument to the newly established UNESCO, Lévi-Strauss recommended that Europe give up its belief in the existence of a set of absolute cultural values and endorse the idea of cultural relativism instead. With his remarks the anthropologist called into question the founding philosophical assumptions of this international cultural organization. As Finkielkraut summarized the problem: "Enlighten humanity to avoid the risk of falling back into barbarism, Lévi-Strauss endorsed the solemn goal of the founders of UNESCO, but turned against the philosophy that inspired it. . . . The objective remained the same: destroy prejudice, but to achieve this goal, it was no longer a matter of opening others to reason, but of opening ourselves to the reason of others."

Finkielkraut also challenges theorists of national liberation for claiming to offer a non-Western alternative when what they are doing is evoking the *Volksgeist.* But by raising the issue,

Finkielkraut poses serious questions about the cultural dimensions of democratic theory as well. He invites us to think, for example, about the implications of supporting international organizations that exempt human rights from debates about cultural autonomy. Third world leaders have exposed the contradictions implicit in taking such a stand and frequently reject the authority of human rights groups on cultural grounds. Yet some Western proponents of cultural relativism want it both ways. While championing the cause of cultural diversity, they firmly believe that all nations should establish human rights legislation based on Western assumptions of what these rights entail. Thus they find themselves in the curious position of criticizing the Eurocentric ideals of the Enlightenment, while promoting a universalistic definition of human rights that adheres closely to the liberal democratic "method" of seventeenth- and eighteenth-century England and France, a method that purported to transcend cultural specificities and create a set of abstract laws applicable to all peoples.

The philosophical method, Tocqueville claims,

is not only French, but democratic; and this explains why it was so readily admitted throughout Europe, where it has contributed so powerfully to change the face of society. It is not because the French have changed their former opinions and altered their former manners that they have convulsed the world, but because they were the first to generalize and bring to light a philosophical method by the aid of which it became easy to attack all that was old and to open a path to all that was new.[2]

By generalizing, the argument goes, the democratic philosophical method can be applied to every nation seeking to establish political equality before the law for all its citizens, whatever their ethnic or class origins. Establishing the idea of the abstract individual, the democrat identifies a set of basic rights that all peoples should enjoy, no matter who they are or what culture they come from. Blind to difference, however, the democrat "recognizes neither Jew, nor Arab, nor Negro, nor bourgeois, nor worker, but only man—man always the same in all times and all places."[3]

After defining the rights of abstract individuals, philosophers of the French Enlightenment assumed that each and every person would freely choose a national culture. And Finkielkraut firmly supports this idea. Those who elect to become citizens of a democratic state can maintain their own traditions if they wish, but they have an obligation to respect the rights of individuals protected by custom and law. While defending his position, Finkielkraut warns against the other side of the problem: the globalization of aspects of Euro-American culture. In particular he singles out the detrimental effects of consumerism and the cult of the young. Challenging the self-interested values of popular culture in the postmodern West, he exposes the vulgarity of contemporary expressions of our so-called concern for the starving peoples in other parts of the world, like the rock concert given to raise money for Ethiopians..

Writing in the time-honored form of the French essay, Alain Finkielkraut wants to be provocative. And in that he succeeds brilliantly, pushing the reader to take a new look at a controversy long dominated by intractable factions defending untenable positions. By reviewing the philosophical heritage of contemporary debates about multiculturalism and ethnicity, Finkielkraut raises questions singularly missing in American discussions of the issues.

Alain Finkielkraut does not offer the reader a detailed scholarly work on the subject. In writing an essay, he has chosen to outline the problem instead, adopting the forceful, succinct style associated with the form. In the process, he makes his case with broad strokes, boldly arguing his position with no excuses or qualifications. For example, while he draws a sharp contrast between the French Enlightenment and the German Romantic movement, he does not insist on the fact that important disagreements also existed within each philosophical tradition. Nor does he address in any detail the injustices endured by specific groups of people who have lived and still live in democratic nation-states. Nevertheless, despite the sketchlike quality of the text, Finkielkraut defends the abstract individual in French Enlightenment thought persuasively. In the end the democrat, to paraphrase Jean-Paul Sartre, is the minority person's best friend. As discriminated-against groups in the United States have shown, the "democratic method," with all its limitations, has provided women, blacks, and homosexuals legal ways to challenge the Constitution and make the laws of the land more inclusive.

To give another example, Alain Finkielkraut makes only passing reference to the noble origins of cultural relativism. But here too his analysis holds. Franz Boas, it is true, introduced the idea in the early years of this century, first as part of a campaign to combat the Eugenics movement in the United States, then as one to challenge the rise of National Socialism in Europe. Since those early days, however, many anthropologists have objected to the ways political and economic interest groups have used cultural relativism to defend a troubling array of policies and goals.[4] Finkielkraut contributes to the discussions taking place within the discipline by linking the misuses made of cultural relativism to similar misuses of the *Volksgeist*; also by insisting that we analyze together the underlying assumptions of the two concepts.

The Defeat of the Mind was published in France in 1987. It appeared in an English translation a year later.[5] What follows here is a new translation. Although I consulted and benefited from Dennis O'Keefe's earlier achievement, the American edition is significantly different from the British. Whenever possible I have provided the reader with references to published translations in English of the many citations from other languages included in the text. Frequently, however, I have reworked the translations for stylistic purposes.[6]

A final editorial note: after giving the matter a good deal of thought, I decided not to follow any of the conventions currently in use to neutralize the gender of the third-person singular pronoun. *The Defeat of the Mind* embraces a tradition that created the ideal of the abstract individual: where *he* stood uncontested for both *him* and *her*.

New York
August 1994

Notes

1. For a more complete review of Finkielkraut's intellectual and political evolution, see Judith Friedlander, *Vilna on the Seine: Jewish Intellectuals in France Since 1968* (New Haven: Yale University Press, 1990). Finkielkraut's book on the trial of Klaus Barbie has been published by Columbia University Press in the same series as *The Defeat of the Mind*. See *Remembering in Vain: The Klaus Barbie Trial and Crimes Against Humanity*, trans. R. Lapidus with S. Godfrey, introduction by Alice Y. Kaplan (1992). Also in English is *The Imaginary Jew*, trans. D. Suchoff (Lincoln: University of Nebraska Press, 1994).

2. Alexis de Tocqueville, *Democracy in America*, trans. H. Reeve, as revised by F. Bowen, 2 vols. (New York: Vintage, 1954), 2:6.

3. Jean-Paul Sartre, *Anti-Semite and Jew*, trans. G. Becker (New York: Schocken Books, 1965), p. 55.

4. In my own case I have written about the problem in Mexico. See Judith Friedlander, *Being Indian in Hueyapan: A Study of Forced Identity in Contemporary Mexico* (New York: St. Martin's, 1975).

5. Finkielkraut, *The Undoing of Thought*, trans. D. O'Keefe (London: Claridge Press, 1988).

6. I would like to thank Lindsay Dubois for her heroic work in helping me track down published English translations of the many texts cited in Alain Finkielkraut's book. A number of references, however, remain incomplete, for which our apologies. To do better than we did would have required more editorial assistance from Alain Finkielkraut than the author had time to give us. The reader should keep in mind that *La Défaite de la pensée* was published in Gallimard's essay series targeted for a wide public and did not, as a result, have to conform to the conventions traditionally followed by American university presses.

THE DEFEAT OF THE MIND

In a scene in Jean-Luc Goddard's film *Vivre sa vie*, Brice Parain, who plays the role of a philosopher, contrasts everyday life with *the life of the mind*, which he also calls the superior life.

This hierarchical distinction, a basic building block of Western civilization, has always stood on fragile ground. To this day it provokes a great deal of debate. Recently, however, the arguments of those both for and against have taken a new turn. Now they each defend their position by evoking the name of culture. But by culture they mean very different things. One uses the concept to affirm the preeminence of the life of the mind, the other to deny it, claiming that everything is cultural, from simple gestures made in the course of a day, to the creation of masterpieces. Why give preference to one over the other? Why privilege thinking over knitting, or chewing betel nuts, or performing the ancestral morning rite of dunking a piece of thickly buttered toast into a cup of hot coffee?

There is a feeling of malaise in our cultural life. No one, it is true, is likely to pull out a gun upon hearing the word—but more people than ever are reaching for their culture to challenge the "life of the mind." This book tells the story of the rise and triumph of these people.

PART ONE

·

THE IDEA OF THE SPIRIT TAKES ROOT

The *Volksgeist*

In 1926 Julien Benda published *The Treason of the Intellectuals*. His subject: "a cataclysm of moral notions in those who educate the world."[1] Benda worried about the enthusiastic interest European intellectuals were taking in the mysterious depths of the collective soul. He criticized the way those selected to carry on the work of the mind had turned against their ancient calling with ecstasy, repudiating universalism and glorifying particularisms, focusing on those qualities that made one people different from another. Benda noted with astonishment that contemporaries of his in the scholarly community had abandoned their concern for upholding eternal values. Instead, they offered their talent and prestige to the service of provincial causes, stirring up xenophobic sentiments, calling upon their nation to love and adore only themselves, to present themselves "against all other nations as superior in language, art, literature, philosophy, civilization, 'culture.'"[2]

For Benda this transmutation from culture *in general* to *my* culture *in particular* was the true mark of the modern period, its critical and irreplaceable contribution to the moral history of humankind. Culture had once been the domain in which the spiritual and creative life of man developed. It had now become my culture, the mentality of the people to whom I belonged, a spirit imbued with my loftiest thoughts and the simplest gestures of my daily existence. This second meaning of culture, as Benda himself made clear, had roots in German Romanticism.

The concept of the *Volksgeist*, or spirit of the people, first appeared in 1774, in Herder's "Yet Another Philosophy of History Concerning the Development of Mankind." [3] Taking Montesquieu's thesis from *The Spirit of the Laws*—"A number of things govern men: climate, religion, law, the conventions of government, the influence of past things, customs and manners. All these conspire to form a general outlook or mentality."— and radicalizing it, Herder claimed that all nations, from the most exalted to the most humble, had a unique way of being that could not be interchanged one with the other. Whereas Montesquieu had taken care to maintain the distinction between positive laws and universal principles of equity, Herder did not. Nothing had higher authority for Herder than the plurality of collective souls. All supranational values, whether legal, aesthetic, or moral, had lost their sovereignty.

Herder wanted to put an end to the idea he deemed false, that you could evaluate human creations out of context, remove them from the place where they had been produced, and judge them according to timeless criteria of what is Good, True, or Beautiful. Instead of measuring facts by a set of ideal norms, he showed that the norms themselves had not always existed. They too belonged to a particular context, to a history that began at some point in time. Put another way, these norms were nothing more than facts themselves. Herder sent the eternal Good, True, and Beautiful back to their place of birth, throwing them out of Heaven where they had basked in the

Glory, returning them to earth and their more humble origins. There was no absolute, Herder proclaimed—only regional values and contingent principles. Far from being of all times and all places, each historical period and nation corresponded to a specific type of humanity. Socrates: an Athenian of the fifth century before Jesus Christ. The Bible: a poetic expression of the Hebrew soul over several periods. All that was Divine was human; even the Word belonged to history.

In contrast to the ancients, who attributed no importance to the passage of time, Herder believed that change mattered and joined contemporaries of his in analyzing the role of history. But unlike the moderns who sought to conquer the realm of history armed with universal norms, Herder refused to use the same weapons; he did not, for example, accept the distinction between reason and custom. For Herder Voltaire's idea that reason would progressively win out over custom and prejudice made as little sense as the classical image of an eternal cycle of violence and crime. One could not, Herder said, dissociate history from reason and denounce with monotonous indignation—the way the moralists did—the savagery and folly of humankind. Nor could one follow those eighteenth-century philosophes and try to make the future conform to reason, measuring—as they did—the laborious, continuous, linear movement of civilization. It was not history that was reasonable, or even rational, it was reason that was historical: of the many forms of humanity engendered over time, each possessed their independent existence, their immanent necessity, their individual reason.

This philosophy called for a methodology directly opposed to the one recommended by Voltaire. Instead of molding infinitely flexible human beings into one supposedly identical or uniform type, instead of "uprooting some particular Egyptian virtue from its place and time, that is from the infancy of the human imagination, and then trying to show its worth in terms of another era," one had to compare like with like: an Egyptian virtue with an Egyptian temple, Socrates with his compatriots and men of his time, not with Spinoza or Kant.

According to Herder Voltaire's blindness reflected the arrogance of his nation. If his thinking was false, if, incorrectly, he brought together a multiplicity of historical situations, he did so because he believed in the superiority of his country (France) and in the period in which he lived (the Enlightenment). Judging history in light of what he called reason, he committed the sin of being arrogant, of attributing eternal dimensions to a particular and time-bound way of thinking. Voltaire demonstrated the same conquering spirit in his desire to "dominate the whole vast extent of all peoples of all times and places" and—in keeping with the goals of French rationalism—to expand France's borders beyond their national limits and subjugate the rest of the world. Voltaire interpreted past historical events according to the official views of his country, fastening French intellectual shackles on other European nations, notably Germany. Basically, Voltaire imposed on the analysis of historical time the same work of *forced assimilation* the Enlightenment had already applied to space. In a single blow Herder wanted to correct this mistake and combat imperialism, to deliver history from the principle that everyone was the same and return to each nation a sense of pride in being different. If he ardently tried to establish transcendent principles in historical facts, he did so only to rob them for good of the intimidating powers gained from their exalted position. Since prophets spoke only for those in their country, people stopped caring for anyone but themselves. Nothing, no eternal ideal or value independent of time and place, should be allowed to impair the individuality of a people or divert the spirit, the genius, they carried within them. "Let men speak well or ill of our nation, our literature, our language: they are ours, they are ourselves, and let that be enough."[4]

From the beginning or, to be more precise, from the time of Plato to that of Voltaire, human diversity was judged in the court of fixed values. Then came Herder, who turned things around. He had universal values condemned in the court of diversity.

But Herder was a loner. In 1774 Frederick II was king and the Enlightenment enjoyed considerable prestige. The idea of the Volksgeist would only catch on after Prussia's retreat from Jena and Napoleon's subsequent occupation of the country. Broken up into a multitude of principalities, Germany regained its sense of unity through the Volksgeist. It was the Germans' response to a conquering France. The exaltation felt by this collective identity compensated for their military defeat and degrading subjugation, the penalty they had to pay for losing the war. The nation found solace from the humiliation it was suffering through the marvelous discovery of its culture.

To forget their powerlessness they embraced everything Teutonic with a passion. In the name of German specificity they rejected the universal values of the French used to justify the hegemony of France.

Legal scholars and poets made it their mission to affirm this German ancestry. Lawyers enthusiastically endorsed traditional solutions—customs, maxims, and sayings—as the basis for German law, seeing these as a collective work, the unintentional and silent fruits of the spirit of the nation. Poets defended this national spirit against the insertion of foreign ideas. They looked to purify the language by replacing German words that had Latin roots with others thoroughly Germanic. They sought as well to uncover the riches buried in popular songs and, by singing them, make folklore the model of the state of innocence, freshness, and perfection, where the individuality of the people—not yet ruined by foreign contact—still expressed itself in unison.

Enlightenment philosophers defined themselves as "the peaceful legislators of reason."[5] Masters of truth and justice, they made a distinction between despotism, and other abuses, and the equity of an ideal law. German romantics did just the opposite: privileged trustees of the Volksgeist, legal scholars and writers challenged the idea of universal reason or ideal law. In the name of culture they no longer sought to push back prejudice and ignorance but to convey the unique soul of the people, whose guardians they were, in all its impressive singularity.

Declining Humanity in the Plural

During the same period France was recovering from the trauma of the Revolution, and traditionalist thinkers accused the Jacobins of having desecrated the national spirit with abstract theories.

Revolutionaries, it is true, had destroyed the ancien régime with their cry "Long live the nation!" Yet when they introduced the new collective subject, they did not celebrate the originality of its soul, but the equality with which it would rule. In the words of Sieyès: "What is a nation? A body of associates living under common laws and represented by the same legislative assembly."[6] With a single word—*associates*—revolutionaries erased a thousand years of social and political relationships. And in the name of the nation they brutally did away with national history. Class divisions were abolished: no more noblemen, priests, judges, commoners, or peasants; only individual people who enjoyed the same rights and were subject to the same duties. With one word Sieyès proclaimed the end of the hereditary system. To demand special rights by virtue of ancestry excluded one from the nation. So did attempts to try to blend in by evoking a common spirit. Put another way, in saying, "Long live the nation!" the revolutionaries did not go to the trouble of pitting Frenchmen of ordinary stock against blue-blooded nobility or of replacing those concrete qualities that traditionally served to classify and separate people with an entirely new idea of nation, merely to endow the French people with a new spirit. Nor did they dissolve laws acknowledging superiority by birth or do away with titles, positions, and ancestral lineages, simply to turn around and force everyone to identify with their native land. Empirical determinations of this kind no longer made a difference—not even ethnicity.

Going against the etymology of the word (in Latin *nascor* means "I am born"), the revolutionary nation cut people off at the root, defining individuals by their humanity, not by their place of birth. This revolutionary project had no intention of trying to create a collective identity for people who had lost their way. On the contrary: by setting them free of all definitive ties, it radically affirmed their autonomy.

Liberated from ancestral and other kinds of ties, they freed themselves as well from the transcendent authority that had ruled over them. From this time forward they depended neither on God nor family; relying no more on Heaven than they did on heredity. Associates instead of subjugated people, they were *represented*, Sieyès said, by the same legislature. The very power that ruled them had legitimacy because it evolved out of a decision by the people to live together and establish common institutions. A contract determined the exercise of this power, defining both its nature and limits. In sum, government was a good that belonged to the whole nation, whose princes were never more than its "usufructuaries, ministers, or guardians." Even before the Revolution Diderot noted in *The Encylopedia* that if a monarch made bad use of the political authority conferred on him by contract, if he treated this public good as a private good, the nation had the right to relieve him of his office like "a minor who would have acted without full knowledge of the facts."[7] Power, in other words, no longer came from on high but from below, from that union of wills of the people who formed the national collective.

Thus, by opposing aristocratic privilege and the absolute

power of kings, the concept of the nation burst into history. No longer willing to accept a view of society and an understanding of power in which social distinctions existed by virtue of birth, and the monarchy by divine right, the French Revolution substituted the ideal of a free and voluntary association.

For conservatives this was precisely the original sin, the fatal *presumption* that inevitably led to the disintegration of the social fabric, the reign of terror, and, finally, the Napoleonic dictatorship. By coming together to write a constitution, the revolutionaries believed they were recreating the primordial agreement with which society began. In establishing a government by assembly, they thought they had the authority of a social contract. Well and good, replied the defenders of tradition, but there never was a social contract! Citizens did not belong to their nation by virtue of a decree of their sovereign will. This idea was a wild dream, and it led to all kinds of crimes. "No assembly of men," wrote Joseph de Maistre, "can constitute a nation. An attempt of this kind ought even to be ranked among the most memorable acts of folly."[8]

For, as far back as history went, de Maistre continued, people were born into societies already formed, not the other way round. *From the beginning* they had to accommodate their behavior to customs already existing, just as they had to find ways to speak and express their thoughts in languages they did not create and over which they had no power. From the very beginning, whether we speak about language or nation, people entered into a game whose rules they had nothing to do with establishing but had to learn and respect all the same. This went for political constitutions as well as for the agreement of the past participle or for the word used to say *table*. On the one hand, rules varied from nation to nation, on the other, they were fixed; you did not make them up along the way. They developed spontaneously, organically, and unintentionally. Far from corresponding to an explicit will or a deliberate agreement, they grew and ripened imperceptibly in the fertile soil of the nation. You could not trace these rules to a plan clearly conceived by one or more people any more than you could trace the origin of a grammatical rule:

What is a constitution? Is it not the solution to the following problem? Given the population, customs, religion, geography, and political practices of a nation, its wealth and its good and bad qualities, a constitution must identify the laws that correspond to the particularities of the nation. This problem cannot be solved by people relying on their own resources. For every nation this is the patient work of centuries.[9]

Following this line of argument what the revolutionaries did by choosing to *create* a universal constitution was as absurd as if they had declared the French language obsolete and substituted by decree an artificial tongue that all peoples would use. Creating instead of collecting, seeking universal solutions instead of relying on the practices of their own country, these barbaric speculators, drunk on their own theories, endowed their insignificant little selves with godlike powers and prescribed general remedies for a specific situation. Rather than humbly recognize that the problem was beyond their reach, they considered themselves capable of solving it and went about doing their best to destroy their heritage. With disastrous determination, a frenzy of abstraction, and Promethean madness, they quite simply usurped power and ravaged the unique aspects of their history, all in the name of returning political authority to the nation. Coming together to give the collectivity a so-called rational foundation, they cut themselves off from their tradition: they deprived their nation of its creative forces, its singularity; they stripped it of its power in order to destroy its soul. Just when they thought they were liberating the country from outdated institutions that kept them dependent, they betrayed, in fact, their nation's identity in favor of a dream, a purely imaginary idea called Man.

When revolutionaries evoked the name of the nation, it was, we have seen, in order to transfer to man powers that the age-old alliance of throne and altar had reserved for God. A century before Spengler and his *Decline of the West*, conservatives were saying that the idea of man was a figment of the imagination, "a zoological phantom."[10] Only different ways of thinking and national cultures existed. As Joseph de Maistre proclaimed, in one of his famous observations, "There is no such thing as *man* in the world. In my lifetime, I have seen Frenchmen, Italians, Russians. Thanks to Montesquieu, I even know that *one can be Persian*. But as for *man*, I declare that I have never in my life met him; if he exists, he is unknown to me."[11]

Nation against nation the traditionalists challenged the idea of free association, preferring instead an all-encompassing totality. Rejecting Rousseau's model of the general will, they introduced the concept of the collective unconscious—even if they did not yet call it by this name. Curiously, however, the traditionalists still joined the apostles of popular sovereignty in describing legitimate power from the bottom up. Although we might have expected them to dismiss this democratic principle, traditionalists embraced it enthusiastically, but in doing so they placed the nation *below* the individual. From their point of view the revolutionaries did not dig down far enough as they looked for the roots of the collective life. Having assumed that they, the revolutionaries, represented the bottom, they thought they had the right to constitute society. In doing so they forgot the constituent power of society itself. Human subjects did not consciously create the community in which they lived; they were formed, on the contrary, by the community itself, without their ever having been aware of it. It was not the will of its members that created the nation; it was the nation itself that imposed its will on those who belonged to it. Since people were the work of their nation, the product of their environment, and not the other way round, as Enlightenment philosophers and their Republican disciples believed, *human beings had to be declined in the plural*: they were nothing more than the sum of their particular parts, the sum of all those who had peopled the earth. And here de Maistre joined Herder in saying: "Nations have a general overriding *soul* or character and a true moral unity which makes them what they are. This unity is first and foremost determined by language."[12]

And so, what had once been seen as the thoughtful joining together of individuals had now become a matter of unconscious choice. The nation—by means of its social organization and language—introduced meanings and forms to the experience of man that were older than he and that he, as an individual, could never be sure he had mastered. Whether he defined himself as a social being or thinking subject, man was not of his own making, but belonged to something else. He no longer enjoyed the position of *author*, a status assigned to him by the philosophes. In the spirit of counterrevolutionary doctrine, the time had come to wipe the slate clean and return to God His privileged station. If human beings were merely tied to already constituted nations, then the Creator could take credit for the appearance and flourishing of national identities. We could attribute to God that dynamism which gave life to human communities precisely because this force was anonymous, because it was a "process without a subject." Since languages and societies had no identifiable human creators, traditionalists believed they had proved irrefutably that God existed.

And the madman who, defying the order of things, got into his head the idea of establishing a government or creating institutions sinned both against his people and divine will. To the crime of treason he added the sin of blasphemy. It was God Himself whom he offended when he repudiated ancient traditions or garbled national dogmas.

But this God occupied a different place and defined Himself in an entirely new way. While preserving the ancient name of Master of the Universe, the reactionary and theocratic traditionalists of the period used the Deity to close the unfortunate historical parenthesis opened in 1789. They made it their goal to bring back the idea of divine right. But what they called God was no longer the Supreme Being, but collective reason. Identified with tradition, as expressed by the spirit of each people, their God abandoned the celestial heights of Sovereign Grace for the obscure and subterranean reaches of the unconscious. From now on God existed within human intelligence, not beyond it, guiding people's actions and shaping their thoughts without their knowing it. Instead of communicating with all creatures, as His namesake did, by means of the Revelation, God no longer spoke *to* man in a universal tongue; He now spoke from *within* him, in the language of his nation.

De Maistre and Bonald had the same ambition as the classical theoretician of absolutism, Bossuet: to teach people to be submissive, to give them the religion of established power. Or, to borrow Bonald's formulation, to substitute "the evidence of authority for the authority of evidence." But the analogy stopped there: Bossuet wanted to connect human beings to a transcendent order while de Maistre and Bonald, like the German political romantics, sought to establish an innate order. Behind the appearance of a simple return to the past, the counterrevolution abolished all transcendental values, divine as well as human. The abstract individual and the superterrestrial God were subsumed at the same time into the soul of the nation, its culture.

The traditionalists denounced with fanatic fervor the tendency to do critical analyses of religion. For them, there was no greater blasphemy than to make the mysteries of the Scripture fit the criteria of clear and reasonable thought. They therefore went to great lengths to control feelings of doubt and put reason in chains ("the crowning achievement of reasoning is to discover the point at which one must stop thinking"[13]) in order to return to the weakened word of God the supreme authority it once exercised over man. Enough of this playing around, causing thought, art, and daily life to sink into the depths. The time had come to subject people once again to the salutary torments of religious anxiety. Just as before the heavens above must be on the horizon, be the ultimate goal of all human activities. Paradoxically, however, *this return to religion required the destruction of metaphysics.*

The eighteenth century, it is true, was a time of critical questioning and militant impiety, an accursed period when Diderot could say that it mattered a great deal to be able to tell the difference between parsley and hemlock but very little as to whether God existed or not. Still, the Age of Enlightenment was also a metaphysical century, and this made sense. If the philosophes challenged the power of custom, it was because they respected abstract and timeless principles. If they were not afraid to "ride roughshod over prejudice, tradition, antiquity, popular opinion, authority—in a word everything which subjugates the mass of minds"[14]—it was because they, following Plato, elevated the Good above all other existing things. Taking distance at first from the immediate facts, they judged the established order by an unconditional norm, a fixed and immovable idea of what was right.

The counterrevolutionaries refused to follow the revolutionaries to these heights and invoke other abstractions and immaculate doctrines that would challenge those recommended. Instead, they reduced pure ideas to flimsy illusions and established a program for sending the Good off to a place in the future. Their unrelenting hatred of this iconoclastic period, with its absence of faith or dogma, had less to do with the materialism of the time than with its tendency to overindulge in speculation, its taste for metaphysical/moral "clouds." Put another way, they vigorously opposed the influence of Plato on the Enlightenment.

The traditionalists wiped the slate clean of all abstractions. In their struggle against excesses in critical thinking, in their concern for bringing reason back to reason, that is, to respect traditional values, they struck down all dualisms. Eternity no longer stood opposed to time, nor essence to existence, the possible to the real, the intelligible to the impressionable—not even the world above to the world below. Their intensely immanent way of thinking recognized only tangible facts that could be known concretely through history.

These strange, devout people took pains to denounce the illusion of an afterlife. While speaking in defense of a threatened religion, they actually anticipated the nihilism of Nietzsche. According to them philosophy's "original sin" was not the absence of piety but the failure to embrace a sense of history.[15] The religion they observed was the cult of facts: the good is what is. Excellence is a pleonasm for existence. The value of institutions was no longer determined by how closely they approximated an ideal but by their age. Customs gained legitimacy just by being very old. The more ancient the social order, the more it deserved to live on. If a widely held belief came down through the centuries, it did so because it was true. No rational argument could compete with the patina of age, with the consecration of time itself. Having done away with metaphysics, truth only existed in the durability of things.

The Maternal Warmth of Prejudice

Herder said:

Prejudice is good in its time and place, because it makes people happy. It takes them back to their center, attaches them firmly to their roots, lets them flourish in their own way, makes them more impassioned, and, as a result, happier in their inclinations and purposes. The most ignorant nation, the one with the most prejudices, is often superior in this respect. When people dream of emigrating to foreign lands to seek hope and salvation, they reveal the first symptoms of sickness and flatulence, of approaching death.[16]

De Maistre said:

All known nations have been happy or powerful to the degree they have faithfully obeyed this national mind, which is nothing other than the destruction of individual dogmas and the absolute and general rule of national dogmas, that is to say, useful prejudices.[17]

In declaring their love of prejudice, the French counterrevolutionaries and the German romantics rehabilitated the most pejorative word in the language of the Enlightenment. And, as if that were not enough, they added insult to injury by dignifying the term and calling it culture. Challenging the assumption that obscurantism flourished when individual reason slept, they saw this as a time when collective reason developed. Prejudices constituted the cultural treasure of every nation: the presence of "we" in the "I," the past in the present, revered vessels of popular memory, judgments transmitted from century to century, ancient secrets preceding consciousness, the guardians of thought. In the eyes of their critics, under the pretext of spreading enlightenment, the philosophes worked furiously to obliterate these precious remains. Instead of cherishing them, they wanted them destroyed. And not content to do it by themselves, they called on the people to help. As Kant wrote, they chose as their motto: *Sapere aude*, do not be afraid to know, be brave and challenge conventions, "have the courage to act as you see fit," without the help of a guide to your conscience or the crutch of received ideas. And what was the outcome? Enlightenment thinkers tore people away from their culture at the very moment they claimed to be educating them; they chased history away in the name of banishing superstition or error. Instead of emancipating souls, as they thought they had done, they succeeded in uprooting them. These commonplace slanderers had not freed understanding from its chains but cut it off at its roots. Thanks to the philosophes, individuals who had now become adults (i.e., citizens of a democracy with full responsibility) found themselves emptied of their very being. In becoming the cause of the struggle, they had abandoned themselves. Striving for independence, they had lost all substance; the promises of *cogito* proved false. Emancipated from prejudice, removed from national beliefs, the subject did not become free, but shriveled up and lost all vitality, like a tree deprived of its sap.

The ideas of everyday life should therefore be seen as the soil in which thinking grows. They were the home, the origin, the womb. From these sources thinking emerged and not, as the philosophes would have us believe, from some foreign authority that overwhelmed and flattened local points of view. The traditionalists summed up the Age of Enlightenment as a fatal misunderstanding: the philosophes, they said, had made a mistake about the nature and, one might add, the sex of prejudice. They had turned a nurturing mother, who embraced and inspired us, into a father who beat us. Then, in seeking to overthrow the father, they killed the mother. This murder, intended to liberate, plunged mankind into misery and confusion, as the revolutionary cataclysm demonstrated.

Values had to change. Eager to make philosophy popular with everyone, Diderot wanted the people to share the philosophers' worldview. But that was the opposite of what was needed. The philosophes had to move closer to popular wisdom, place thought in the school of common opinion, sink the *cogito* into the profound depths of the collectivity, renew broken ties with former generations, replace the quest for autonomy with one for authenticity, abandon a critical stance and turn everyone over to the comforting warmth of the ideas and infallible judgment of the majority, link reason to instinct. In other words, for the sake of the nation, one should abandon this "great society of intellects spreading everywhere and everywhere independent"[18] that Enlightenment thinkers had taken such pride in establishing. By restoring primitive unity to society, the counterrevolutionaries had the pleasure of knowing with exalted certainty that they would live once again in truth.

"Was He not struck by the nonsense of the world's wisdom?" Saint Paul used to ask of God, whose apostle he had become. Since the dawn of Christianity mystics or theologians have always come along to proclaim the life of the mind as part of the curse religion has put on human existence. Their judgment stemmed from the conviction that every natural act was a sin and that the exercise of reason was a natural act. Hopelessly corrupted, man could only engage in crime and wickedness. Tainted as he was by original sin, the products of his mind were contaminated. Left to his own devices, he was as incapable of lucidity as he was of greatness. Only a word from on high could release him from his own baseness and free him from the evils of the flesh. From this point of view, there was no intermediate zone between the lascivious desires of human beings and the charity of God. Our fall from Grace affected every aspect of human existence. Any thought of an independent intellectual life was an illusion, prompted by pride.

But despite appearances and the invectives spewed forth in disgust at the revolutionary period, the traditionalists did not subscribe to this pessimistic view of humanity. Without saying so publicly—perhaps without even being fully aware—they broke with the vision of the world they claimed to have inherited. As we have seen, the lost abilities and virtues they wanted restored did not come from God but from the spirit of the nation. Everyone was imbued with the special substance of their people, shaped by their idiom in all domains, from the forms of their religious practice to their most natural impulses.

According to the counterrevolutionaries, human nature as a universalistic construct had no more possibility of existing than did an autonomous spiritual life. Responding to Descartes, they said: I think, therefore I am from somewhere; by exercising my powers of reflection, I do not affirm my sovereignty, I betray my identity. And this repudiation of the *cogito* extended to acts of charity and lascivious desires. These forms of behavior also belonged to the realm of society, as facts whose true subject was the collectivity. These distinct parts of reality gathered together under a national banner and became known by what the German romantics called the Volksgeist. The critique of the revolutionary nation provided as well the arguments needed to attack French cosmopolitanism.

And this discovery turned the intellectual landscape upside down. The name the traditionalists chose for themselves should not lead us astray. Inspired by a passion for the past, German romantics and French theocrats accomplished nothing less than a veritable epistemological revolution. Their hatred of modernity led them to conceive of a radically new view of man. Their nostalgia gave way to a mutation in thought that has continued to influence us to the present day. In spite of themselves these relentless defenders of the past were inventors of something new. In their mania to restore man to his proper place, they discovered unconscious thought, which worked from within. And in so doing they founded the social sciences.

The traditionalists may have left the political and intellectual scene rather quickly, but philologists, sociologists, and historians moved in immediately. Taking up the baton, they continued to make the case for the Volksgeist as they participated in the ongoing debate about the two types of nation—the one proposed by the French revolutionaries and the other by the German romantics. From then on scholars, not ideologues, declared that the social contract was a fiction, because autonomous individuals did not exist outside society.[19]

All of a sudden everything got turned around, and those defending rationalism changed sides. The sciences of the unconscious uncovered the logic of laws and beliefs that the philosophes had unwisely made fun of. They caught the Enlightenment in the act of committing the crime of intellectual blindness. By treating history as the fundamental mode of human existence, by showing how values changed in society over time—those needed in one period would eventually run their course—by replacing the criticism of popular opinion with objective studies on how this opinion evolved, the positivists turned the charge of superstition and ignorance back on the "enlightened minds" of the eighteenth century. Previously the philosophes felt obliged to emancipate their people from such fanciful concepts as divine right; now, with the rise of social sciences, their ideas about the social contract and natural law were rejected as myths. In place of impassioned declarations by de Maistre and Herder came the sarcastic observations of scholars, who, in an ironic twist of fate, imposed on philosophy the humiliation the latter once inflicted on religion: this phantasmagoric vision of the world, Taine wrote with scorn, assumed that "Men born at twenty-one years of age, without family, past or tradition; without duty, without a country, are going to be gathered together for the first time and are going to deal with each other."[20]

We often speak about the beginning of the liberal order in Europe as a victory of progress over reaction, the result of a long and precarious conflict between the forces of modernity and the persistence of the ancien régime. To do so is to forget the main problem the republicans faced throughout the nineteenth century, namely to remain loyal to the Enlightenment while recognizing as well the *progress* of knowledge, to rely on natural rights without denying the *scientific* value of what Joseph de Maistre had established: "Every question about the *nature* of man must be resolved by history."[21] In sum, republicans had to find a way out of sounding like backward metaphysicians as they confronted the positivist ideas issuing forth from the counterrevolution.

What Is a Nation?

One event, however, made it difficult for science to give the Volksgeist its blessing: the Franco-Prussian War of 1870, more precisely, the conquest of Alsace-Lorraine by the Germans. This episode not only stirred up nationalist passions, it reawakened the controversy about whether to define a nation as the inner spirit of the people or as a contract made between individuals. Beyond popular expressions of patriotism—cartographers who shaded in eastern France on their maps with black ink as a sign of mourning or children who learned to sing *O Tannenbaum* on Christmas Eve in honor of little Alsatians or batallions of students, with bayonets in their hands and berets with red pompoms on their heads, marching to "You have taken Alsace and Lorraine / But you will never win our hearts"[22]—beyond this folklore, the dispute over borders provoked a philosophical debate of major importance.

From the moment the fighting was over leading German historians used scientific arguments to justify the annexation of new territories. Refusing to separate man from his origins, seeking the truth about his being and the key to his behavior in those forces that governed him without his knowledge—language, race, historical tradition—they noted with authority that the Alsatians spoke German and belonged to the German culture. The conquest, they concluded, was legitimate: "The Alsatians are of our stock, therefore they belong to us," Strauss and Mommsen affirmed. "The cultural community gives reason for taking the land. French rule tore these provinces away from their true family. The Prussian victory corrects this historical anomaly and permits [the inhabitants of Alsace and Lorraine] to return to the bosom of their nation."

When Strauss and Mommsen used the prestige of the university to back the actions of a victorious Germany, their French counterparts felt that they had to respond immediately. They replied, however, on entirely different grounds. Instead of trying to demonstrate the Celtic origins of the people living in the stolen provinces, instead of making an overblown case based on philological and ethnographic details, they willingly conceded that Alsace was German in language and race. But, Renan added,

it did not want to belong to the German State. And that is the real issue. We are speaking here about the rights of France and the rights of Germany. The rights of living Alsatians touch us more than these [ethnographic] abstractions; the rights of people with flesh and blood to submit to the power of their choice.[23]

Fustel de Coulanges went on in the same vein: "Neither race nor language distinguishes one nation from the other. Men feel in their hearts that they belong to the same people when they share ideas, interests, affections, memories and hopes. That is what makes a nation. . . . Our nation is the place we love."[24]

Before the crisis, however, Renan and Fustel de Coulanges shared the German historians' scorn for the naive anthropology of the Enlightenment. They believed it went without saying that individuals belonged to a nation based on their heredity and on the language they spoke, not the other way round, as the dangerous sophists of the preceding century had proclaimed. In the early days after the defeat, Renan was still blaming "the false politics of Rousseau"[25] for the outcome of the war. According to him the Revolution ruined France by squandering its national heritage in the name of a specious conception of the nation: "The day when France beheaded her king, she committed suicide."[26]

The contrast between the will of the Alsatians and their ethnic origins forced Renan to reconsider his position. As early as the armistice and even before negotiations began at Versailles between France and the new German Empire, deputies from Alsace and Lorraine affirmed their loyalty to France in the National Assembly: "We proclaim the right of the people of Alsace and Lorraine to remain members of the French nation, and we swear, for us, for those we represent, for our children and their descendants, to uphold this right forever, and by whatever means necessary, from within and against all usurpers." And they repeated their claim immediately after the loss of the two provinces and the ratification of this fact by the Assembly:

Once again we declare null and void *the pact which hands us over against our will*. . . . The upholding of our rights remains forever open to each and everyone, in the form and to the extent that our conscience will determine. Your brothers from Alsace and Lorraine, separated from the common family, will maintain their filial love for France, despite her absence from their homes, until such time as she comes back to resume her rightful place.[27]

This outburst of patriotism, in a region where people sang *O Tannenbaum* spontaneously on Christmas Eve, demonstrated without a doubt that language, inherited characteristics, and tradition did not exercise absolute power over individuals as the social sciences had suggested. It proved that people expressed national feelings as a matter of free choice, not as the result of some unconscious determination. In responding the way they did the inhabitants of Alsace-Lorraine made the worn-out idea of the contract meaningful once again in a strange and paradoxical way. The very same Renan who had once rejected as pernicious the idea of an original contract, spoke now of the nation as the object of an *implicit contract* sealed daily by those who belonged to it:

A nation, therefore, is the result of a great sense of solidarity, constituted by the sacrifices people have made and are willing to make. Although it assumes a past, it defines itself in the present by a tangible fact: the agreement, the desire clearly expressed, to continue a life together. The existence of a nation involves a daily plebiscite.[28]

Renan's definition embraced the long history that Sieyès had so carelessly rejected and swept away into the shadows of despotism. In doing so, however, he moved from the formal to the concrete level of living traditions in explaining what gave the nation its particular character. The "body of associates" in *What Is the Third Estate?* had become "an association over the centuries" in *What Is a Nation?* The nation in general became the *French* nation in particular, endowed with a rich history that transcended splits and differences, indivisible and irreplaceable by any other. The year 1789 was an episode in the life of the nation, not the date when the nation emerged from the shadows and threw off its past. Yet in spite of himself, Renan ended up agreeing with the revolutionaries. He may have reestablished the link between social ties in contemporary France and the long history of the country, a bond from which they had been set free, but he concluded all the same that the Volksgeist did not constitute a nation. The organic community of blood, soil, custom, and history did not regulate human behavior, he maintained. Nations came into being through the voluntary association of individuals.

After having made his argument in terms of collective entities, assailing "the appalling simplicity of the Semitic mind which shrinks the human brain, closing out all refined ideas,"[29] and affirming in no uncertain terms that "the Semitic race, compared to the Indo-European race, represents a truly inferior form of human nature,"[30] Renan suddenly and brutally discovered the irreducible character of various kinds of consciousness. In the shock of events the man who had been "the chief scientific sponsor in France of the aryan myth"[31] stopped seeing the spirit as a mental prison. The scientific concepts of race and culture lost their use for Renan, who no longer saw the nation as an entity but more in terms of what Husserl would later call an "intersubjective community."

We all know it is unfair to reduce the question of Alsace-Lorraine to a parochial dispute. To the triumphant ideology of pan-Germanism Renan responded with another theory of the nation, founded on a different conception of man.

According to Strauss and Mommsen man was captive to his history; his personal uniqueness pure illusion. Every part of him—to the innermost recesses of his being—reflected the history he inherited, the language he spoke, the society that gave him life. Tradition arrived before he did; he belonged to his culture before he belonged to himself. For Renan, however, even if there existed a time lag between the rise of a tradition and the consciousness of individual men, a delay that justified establishing the social sciences, human beings, once formed, had the

ability to think: "Let us not abandon this fundamental principle: man is a rational and moral being, before he is closed off in
such and such a language, becomes a member of such and such
a race, the faithful follower of such and such a culture."[32]

From the Renaissance to the Enlightenment the modern
age sought to deliver the human spirit from the revealed truth
and dogmas of the Church. Liberated from established teachings, man became answerable only to reason. He went forth
from childhood (to use Kant's famous formulation) and proclaimed himself ready to think for himself without the help of
his father. Adding another clause to the definition of an adult
man, Renan separated the life of the mind from the community in which it took root. Man had the ability, Renan maintained, to break away, to lift himself out of his context and
escape his national heritage, to speak, think, and create without
bearing witness, necessarily, to the totality from which he came.
In other words, man did not struggle hard to free himself from
the teachings of his father, to be absorbed with no recourse by
a devouring mother: culture. "Before French culture, German
culture and Italian culture, there is human culture."[33]

By insisting on the distinction between national culture and
human culture, Renan made reference implicitly to Goethe,
contrasting the poet's vision of the world with the one introduced by German nationalists.

A Conversation with Eckermann

On January 31, 1827, when Goethe was at the height of his
fame and in the waning years of his life, he spoke to the faith-

ful Eckermann about a Chinese novel he was reading that he found truly remarkable. Although he expected to be struck by the distinctiveness of the work, by its picturesque qualities, he discovered instead similarities to his own epic, *Hermann and Dorothea*, and to the novels of the English writer Richardson.

What surprised him was not the exotic nature of the book, but how familiar it was. Here was this fragment of a distant and little-known civilization that was not at all strange. This intrigued Goethe; the book gave him further evidence that spirit transcended society and history. With this unlikely encounter between himself, the patriarch of Europe, and a Chinese novel, he felt a sense of connection despite all the differences. People had roots to a particular soil, and were tied to a certain time and place, but they could still escape the fate of their specificity, of being defined in national terms. Through books they produced a multiplicity of voices from the same land.

With this marvelous observation Goethe quickly drew up a plan of action. Since literature had the ability to conquer or transcend differences attributed to time, race, or culture, it had the obligation to do so. The possibility of achieving such a goal became his ideal. Reaching this utopia, this nowhere beyond time and place, became his true vocation, leading him to value only those works in which the questions of "where and when?" could not be resolved with certainty.

In order for works like these to proliferate, writers and readers had to open themselves up to a wide range of influences, to have the opportunity to look beyond their immediate surroundings. Hence the importance Goethe placed on the work of translation and on all other forms of literary exchanges. The circulation of forms and ideas, he believed, would put an end to the absolute reign of parochial beliefs, where all inspiration came from within. Thanks to these exchanges peoples would no longer close themselves off at national borders, living as if they inhabited isolated planets. Languages would not be frozen in time. In such a climate works of literature would detach themselves from the land and enter society as individuals, no longer ranked according to origin. Following a period of provincial writing would come the age of world literature: "I like to look around me and therefore at foreign nations and I advise everyone to do the same. The term *national literature* does not mean a great deal anymore; we are moving into an age of world literature and should do all we can to hasten its arrival."[34]

However, a half century earlier, in 1771, the very same Goethe discovered with ecstasy the existence of a specifically German art and literature. At the time he was in Strasbourg, where two events affected him a great deal: meeting Herder and seeing the cathedral.

To find this edifice, built on what was old German soil, during a period entirely German, and to read on a modest tomb the name of the architect, whose name was German in sound and origin, my enthusiasm for this great work of art grew to such proportions that I rejected the infamous term Gothic, which had been used to identify it up until then, and reclaimed it for my country as German architecture.[35]

In Strasbourg, the capital of Alsace and, in this period, a province of France, Goethe had the sudden revelation that great masterpieces expressed national characteristics. German art was distinct. For the first time the aesthetic meaning of "Germany" came to him in all its clarity. What he saw then led Goethe to write "German Architecture." It appeared in 1772 in a collection that included a text by Herder. Goethe's piece summarized his credo with the formulation: "Characteristic art is the only true art."[36] With this statement he challenged the prevailing opinion of the times. The Age of Enlightenment, he maintained, was blind to differences and guilty of rejecting the spirit of individual peoples. It was a period in which nations "sent their children away to gather foreign plants instead of cultivating their own."[37] Would he not himself have joined these lost children if, just as he was leaving Strasbourg to go to Paris—to that Babylon of modernity—a providential monument had not kept him from falling into the cosmopolitan abyss, awakening in him, at the very last minute, a sense of his German identity?

Goethe went on to define Beauty by what, in effect, was typical of the nation, thereby substituting a commitment to the exchange of ideas with one for spiritual autarky. Openness encouraged uniformity of taste in the way people acted and in the works of art they produced; it was better to close in on ourselves and protect human differences. We should reach in, not out, limit contacts, rather than extend them, defend ourselves from foreign influences instead of delighting in them. If there existed no value higher than the unique spirit of each nation, then the writer's work was mapped out for him: imitate the

Strasbourg cathedral, provide the place of his birth with a voice, take hold of the spirit of his people and describe the way it looks.

But Goethe sobered up rather quickly from this inebriated outburst of patriotism. The claims he made in the name of Volksgeist lyricism did not have a lasting effect on him. He soon wrote his contemporaries off, and even went so far as to break with Herder at a time when Germany's intellectuals were succumbing to the soothing charms of the philosopher's thought. When asked in 1808 (two years after Jena) to give an opinion about putting together an anthology of the best poetry in Germany for the benefit of the people, he offered just one piece of advice: include German translations of foreign poems.[38]

To make this suggestion in the midst of the Napoleonic occupation, in an atmosphere of despair and frantic patriotism, was pure provocation. But by doing so Goethe rejected the idea that the artist owed his country allegiance without ever questioning it. While other poets and thinkers praised the mysterious depths of the German soul and offered their services to destroy universalist tendencies, he dared declare:

We will have more success in achieving a degree of general tolerance if we leave undisturbed the distinctive qualities that make individual human beings and whole peoples different and remain true to the idea that the value of anything with true merit lies in its belonging to all humanity.[39]

Thus Goethe renewed his ties to the metaphysical tradition broken off by the Volksgeist, that is, by the systematic nationalization of things of the spirit. And he did so with his eyes open. From Herder he had learned that man did not belong to every period and place, that the language he spoke, the countryside he inhabited, the history into which he had been thrown, were not secondary characteristics or ornaments tacked on by nature. He knew, as we would say today, that man was "situated," that no one escaped the particularities of birth by decree. Still Goethe maintained:

As a man, and a citizen, the poet will love his country, but the land of his poetic strength and inspiration is the Good, the Noble, the Beautiful. And this place belongs to no one province or country. The poet cannot go there, take hold of these qualities and shape them, right where he finds them.[40]

While rejecting the vision of the Volksgeist, Goethe also distinguished himself in radical ways from the classical priests of the Good, the Noble, and the Beautiful. For him ethnicity was not an accidental part of one's existence, it was fundamental and primary.

But Goethe refused—and this is the essential point—to make a virtue out of necessity. We could no longer deny the fact that we reflected a particular tradition, that we had been shaped by our national heritage. However, we should never worship this fact. We should recognize the reality of the situation, not idolize it. By breathing the same air as the other members of the tribe, by being born, like everybody else, into a world with a history and divided loyalties, the artist could not lay immediate claim on universality. He shared spontaneously the same way of seeing and judging things as other members of his people. His personality did not differ at first from the collective personality from which came his first thoughts and the words to express them. But that was no reason to add to the problem by erecting a monument in eternal recognition of the strength of these roots, in celebration of a place and a language. Goethe joined Herder up to a point, agreeing that the spirit was tied to each and every people. He then turned against him, and his own youthful convictions, by devaluing this attachment and giving art the task of transcending this dependence rather than hanging on to it more tenaciously. Individual works must surpass the Volksgeist—they should not be an expression of it. Human culture should never be reduced to the sum of each culture. That was why Goethe invited poets, artists, and thinkers to leave the national arena where Herder and his disciples wanted to confine them.

The Most Dangerous Explosive of Modern Times

Goethe found peace after speaking to Eckermann. He felt time was on the side of world literature. Nationalist fervor was losing ground as the trauma of the Napoleonic conquest receded. Romanticism, as a political movement, had weakened to the extent that it seemed it would never recover. Furthermore, a world market was in the process of being born, putting an end to the tendency of nations to turn in on themselves. No part of the human race could continue to live its history cut off from the interconnections of the world's economy. Only recently seen as impenetrable, national borders had become porous. It did not seem possible to keep creative works separate from the generalized circulation of goods. In 1827, so it seemed, the days of the Volksgeist were numbered.

Yet fifty years later leaders of the German university solemnly chose Herder over Goethe. In their eyes art no longer gave any evidence that the spirit was free (that it had the capacity to transcend circumstances, to break the hold of the collectivity, history, or the homeland). On the contrary, art showed concrete proof of the dependence of the spirit. To those who invoked the rights of people to determine their own destiny, they reminded them of the German character of the Strasbourg Cathedral. What was this monument other than a concrete example of why the Alsatians belonged to Germany? The inhabitants today might oppose annexation. But if we looked at the matter over time immemorial, from the historical past they had inherited, whether they liked it or not their rebellion was childish, a passing bout of bad humor, a whim of no consequence or meaning. People could not dispose of what disposed of them, they could not throw away *their* culture as if it were a piece of clothing. To use Renan's ironic summary of this position, "the Germanic family ... has the right to reclaim its members scattered abroad, even when these members do not want to be reunited with the German people."[41]

With the rise of pan-Germanism the influence of Goethe's teachings disappeared from Germany. Reducing culture to the cult of origins, the Volksgeist triumphed, revealing in the process its totalitarian potential. An entirely new form of authority sprung up from this concept originally introduced—let us not forget—to counter French domination. For the first time it was neither the display of force nor the divine right of the state that opposed the will of individuals. It was their very identity. The people of Alsace served a *master* more despotic than any, in that this one had become part of their very *being*. Instead of appealing to external or transcendent laws and principles, the power to which they had to submit drew its claims from within that interior world of individual identities that constituted the collective soul. Here were subjects literally *embodied* by the oppression that held them victim, obliged to recognize themselves in a state that crushed and brandished them in effigy.

Renan considered this imprisonment the most scandalous aspect of the annexation, and its most disturbing political innovation:

We do not have the right to go around the world measuring the skulls of people and then, taking them by the throat, say, "you are of our blood, you belong to us!" Putting aside anthropological characteristics, there is reason, justice, truth and beauty and these are the same for all of us.[42]

Let us be more precise. As Renan pointed out clearly, there was no difference between specifically cultural and racial arguments, between defending the right of conquest by the Strasbourg Cathedral or by the genetic inheritance of the Alsatians. In both cases, in effect, people had been subjected to an unprecedented act of dispossession. In the name of their very essence, they had lost control over their own destiny. Race or culture, this deeper truth, which they had inherited in spite of themselves, had taken precedence over their conscious desire. This was not all, Renan continued. The national spirit suppressed the individual (dragged down by his group of origin) and humanity (cut up into frozen beings, pulverized into a multitude of ethnic personalities closed in on themselves). And if the negation of the individual produced *a power without limits, full-scale* war gave birth to the dislocation of the human species. In other words, nothing stopped members of a state drunk on the Volksgeist; no moral obstacle stood in their way. Deprived of their innermost being, the subjects of the state could lay no claim on their rights. As far as the enemies were concerned, they belonged to a different species entirely. No need to treat them with humanity. Those in the other camp were no longer the same kind; they would fight without mercy. As Renan put it, Dividing human beings into distinct races, [and doing so] on the basis of a scientific error, since few countries possess truly pure races, can only lead to wars of extermination, to "zoological" wars, if you will permit me, analogous to those found among diverse species of rodents or flesh-eating mammals. This would be the end of that fertile mixture we call humanity, which is composed of many elements, all of them necessary. You have raised a new political flag in the world to take the place of liberalism; this ethnological and archaeological politics of yours will kill you.[43]

Although the conflict in Alsace and Lorraine appeared, on the surface, to be a regional problem of limited consequence,

Renan predicted an imminent fall into barbarism. The beautiful idea of the Volksgeist suddenly took on the aspect of "the most dangerous explosive of Modern Times."[44] What he did not see, however, was the way the cause he defended grew progressively and irresistibly contaminated by the ideas he was fighting. Yet that was the paradox of this Franco-German dispute. As the antagonism itself became more extreme, opposition to the theoretical premises weakened. The more the idea of revenge took hold of the imagination ("Revenge is the queen of France," Maurras used to say), the faster French patriotism began to exalt "the eternal hills" and embrace with the conviction of mystics the importance of having roots in the land.

Renan's complaint against the Germans was that they wanted to remain closed up within their nation, scorning individual rights and threatening to break humanity up into distinct pieces. From the intransigent way the Alsatians responded, he concluded that you could not lock people up within the confines of their ethnic groups. But Barrès succeeded Renan, and the movement to resist the loss of French territory evoked the French spirit. With more passion than before the crisis in Alsace and Lorraine, social scientists attacked the liberal principles of the eighteenth century: "We do not have the right, you say, to go around the world measuring the skulls of people?" Motivated by the scientific imperatives of social anthropology, Vacher de Lapouge dug up skulls by the thousands in the Herault Department to determine their "cephalic index." And to Renan, who thought he could proclaim, "Nation is not synonymous with race,"[45] he replied after ten years of fieldwork,

"We do not become part of a family or nation by decree. We are born with blood that runs through our veins and we have the same blood for the rest of our lives. The individual is suppressed by his race; he is nothing. The race and nation are everything."[46] For Gustave Le Bon, psychology dictated that "the life of a people, the institutions they have, their beliefs, and their arts, are only the visible threads of their invisible soul" and that "each and every people possesses a mental constitution as clearly defined as its anatomical characteristics."[47] Thus, with the help of science, Barrès could urge his compatriots to turn away from the great words *eternal* and *forever*, by giving them the example of a language that offered the possibility of saying: *Es denkt in mir*, "it thinks in me," instead of "I think."

And so, concepts and turns of phrases from the other side of the Rhine helped shape the way the French expressed their hatred of Germans. Rising above all other consideration, having intense feelings against the Germans assured the triumph of German thought. As passions flared, differences between the two peoples disappeared. Hostility toward pan-Germanism led to the imitation of it; rejection of the enemy resulted in mimicry. From now on the two sides spoke the same language. They both favored an ethnic conception of nationhood over an elective one. The harbingers of revenge did not object so much to the idea of race as to the *German* race. In other words, it was not so much the nationalization of culture that gave offense, but the culture of the Other. Writers of the past and present lined up under their respective national flags: Montaigne's country against Kant's—an abyss now separated them. Under the circumstances it was not surprising to read the following response by a student to a question about national renewal:

Once I got over the ecstasy I felt after reading the Slavs and the Germans for the first time, I came to see that all this was very beautiful, but it was not me. I enjoyed these works, but I could not live with them; to tell the truth I did not even enjoy them entirely, because one takes pleasure only in what one can create and if I have within me the ability to write *Bérénice*, I could not have produced *Resurrection*. I abandoned Goethe for Racine and Mallarmé, Tolstoy for Balzac and Stendhal. I felt as if I were realizing myself, taking command, sustaining my life in the sense that those from whom I was taking spiritual nourishment were of my flesh and blood.[48]

Born of the defeat at Sedan and fed on the drama of lost provinces, nationalism in France had become nothing other than the French adaptation of all the themes of the Volksgeist.

Renan solemnly reminded Strauss and his "ultrapatriotic generation" of the existence of universal values. In 1898, that is, less than twenty years after Renan exchanged letters with Strauss, those who believed in absolute truth and abstract reason found themselves in the "anti-French" camp. It was the Dreyfusards who vehemently supported the idea that the nation was an association of individual wills and not an organic totality. They vigorously maintained that man "is not the slave of his race, language, or religion, nor of the course of rivers, or the direction of mountain ranges."[49] But by remaining loyal to the principles Renan had defended in *What Is a Nation?* they faced accusations of betraying the identity of their nation: how dare they consider Dreyfus an autonomous individual, when this "son of Shem" was not at all receptive to the intense feelings we had for our land, our ancestors, our flag, for the meaning of the word *honor;*[50] or accept as genuine his declarations of loyalty when, as Drumont once said, "you cannot improvise a sense of patriotism, it is part of your blood and bones"; or go to great lengths to demonstrate his innocence when he was guilty by virtue of his race; or reason like an intellectual instead of thinking and feeling like a Frenchman? In this way the affair remained on the same philosophical plane as the dispute over Alsace-Lorraine, and from this point on the French nationalists adopted the position of Strauss and Mommsen: Dreyfus was guilty, as the inhabitants of the litigious provinces were German, by virtue of his ethnicity, which determined everything he did.

"The Dreyfus affair," wrote Julien Benda, "played a major role in my intellectual development, for it permitted me to see clearly, like a flash of lightning, the hierarchy of values that make up the very basis of my being and of my organic hatred for the opposing system."[51] Never before, it is true, had the two conflicting ideals of the nation, man and culture, ideals that had been dividing Europe since the French Revolution, confronted each other so directly. Never before did it seem so crucial to resolve the question whether the time had come to put an end to the Enlightenment. By rehabilitating Dreyfus France answered the question in the negative. It preferred, in extremis, a society constituted by contract over one based on the idea of a collective spirit. This was a precarious victory. As Benda noted with concern, the most powerful ideologies of the first half of the twentieth century taught that "a people should form a conception of their rights and duties by studying their particular spirit, history, geographical position, the unique circumstances in which they find themselves; not by following the laws of the so-called eternal and universal conscience of man."[52] And these powerful ideologies, Benda warned, would lead "to the most total and perfect war that the world has ever seen."[53]

PART TWO

·

GENEROUS BETRAYAL

A De-Westernized World

In November 1945 members of the United Nations met in London and officially endorsed creating a special branch of the organization to address questions concerning science and culture. At this preparatory conference, called by the governments of the United Kingdom and France, representatives of about forty countries participated, motivated, for the most part, by the same goal. In the beautiful words of Torres Bodet, the delegate from Mexico, they wanted to find a way "of entering an era of human history distinct from that which has just closed."[1] They came together to create a world order in which no one state could draw a curtain around its population or deliberately indoctrinate, "the minds of the people with a set of rigid narrow ideas,"[2] a period in which a true spirit of peace reigned, because ideas circulated freely from one nation to the next. Instead of being trained like animals, manipulated by totalitarian ideologies, turned into subhuman creatures, people would learn to think for themselves as individuals, to use their own powers of reason.

It was the unparalleled ordeal of Nazism that inspired the founders of UNESCO to establish this special branch of the United Nations. Having gone to war to defeat a regime committed to despotism—the suppression of rights—and obscurantism—the exploitation of prejudice and ignorance—they wanted to see an international organization assume the responsibility of watching over the free expression of ideas and helping to combat doctrines and systems of thought that promoted hatred or justified through science the actions of those with the will to dominate. Its task would involve protecting ideas from the abuses of power and enlightening people in such a way that they could never again be swayed by demagogues and led astray in their thinking.

At the gathering in London government leaders and intellectual authorities spontaneously renewed their ties to the spirit of the Enlightenment by linking the moral progress of humanity to intellectual progress and by making a connection between the obligation to defend *political* freedoms with the need to provide opportunities for *cultural* growth. The new and distinct era they hoped would emerge had philosophical roots in the eighteenth century. As they formulated their plans for UNESCO, their vision reflected the implicit patronage of Diderot, Condorcet, and Voltaire. It was these authors who taught us that if freedom was a universal right, only the enlightened could be said to be free. It was they who, when speaking of the role of government, also insisted on two inseparable demands: respect the autonomy of individuals and provide them with the education they need to be truly autonomous. Condorcet, for example, wrote:

Even when freedom is respected in form and preserved in the book of law, does not the prosperity of all still demand that everyone be capable of recognizing those who are competent to maintain it?

And if a man, out of ignorance, depends on another to decide matters of public concern, can he really call himself free?[3]

In the days following the victory over Hitler, the philosophes seemed to provide the guiding light for those who proposed creating an organization like UNESCO. The founders defined their objective as assuring to all full and equal access to education, the free pursuit of objective truth, and the free exchange of ideas and knowledge. Through this form of cultural cooperation they expected the world to acquire the skills needed to resist future assaults on the dignity of man.

But what man were they talking about? The abstract and universal subject of the Declaration of the Rights of Man and of the Citizen? A reality without substance, a being without a being, a creature without flesh, color, or particular quality, like the one who inhabited the great discourses on universalism? An individual, in other words, stripped of everything that made him different? Once UNESCO began meeting officially as an organization, the agenda shifted imperceptibly. What started out as a critique of fanaticism turned into a critique of the Enlightenment. These challenges to the idea of abstract humanism prolonged and radicalized discussions held previously in London that had originally debated ways to protect the world from doctrines tending to deny the unity of the human race. After legal scholars and men of letters had their say, anthropologists took the floor and made the following argument: if humanism represented humanity as a whole, then it had to demonstrate respect for all human beings by describing the concrete forms of people's existence.

A perfect expression of this point of view was a text prepared by Claude Lévi-Strauss in 1951, at the request of UNESCO. Calling the essay "Race and History," Lévi-Strauss began by stating what he would repeat many times in ritual-like fashion, that there was no good definition of race. Differences that existed among human groups pertained, he wrote, "to geographical, historical and sociological circumstances, not to any specific aptitude linked to the anatomical or physiological constitution of blacks, yellows or whites."[4] What is more, Lévi-Strauss added, we must do more than merely distinguish between traits inherited socially and traits having a biological origin. It was not enough to challenge those who used biology to explain differences among peoples by demonstrating that cultural variation was not genetically determined. We must go further, and oppose every effort to rank differences. The many forms taken by human society over time and space could not be classified along a scale rising to perfection. They were not steps in a *marche triomphale*, "stages in a single developmental scheme, which, starting from the same place, had to converge necessarily at the same point."[5] The temptation we had to place human societies on a scale of values, assigning to ourselves the highest position, was as scientifically false and morally harmful as the desire of others to divide human beings into isolated anatomical/physiological entities.

And, according to Lévi-Strauss, Enlightenment thinkers succumbed to this temptation. Intoxicated by everything taking place in eighteenth-century Europe—the development of knowledge, the progress in technology, and the refinement of

customs—the philosophes accounted for all these achievements by creating the concept of *civilization*. They turned their
condition into a model: their customs became universal apti-
tudes, their values absolute criteria for judging. The European
became master over nature. He saw himself as the rightful
owner, the most interesting being in Creation. In the following
century the newly emerging field of anthropology embraced
this grandiose vision of the rise of civilization and reason, con-
firming, more or less, the dominant role of the West in this evolutionary process. Here, for example, was what Lewis Henry
Morgan wrote in *Ancient Society*: "It can now be assented upon
convincing evidence that savagery preceded barbarism in all
the tribes of mankind, as barbarism is known to have preceded
civilization. The history of the human race is one in source, one
in experience, and one in progress."[6]

Fortified by certainty, Europeans finished their work of col-
onization by the end of the nineteenth century. As a rational
and technologically advanced society, Europe was progress
incarnate, particularly when compared to the other cultures of
the world. Given the differences, conquest seemed to offer the
most expeditious and *generous* way to bring people who
remained so far behind into the orbit of civilization. Advanced
nations had a mission: to hasten the march of non-Europeans
toward a life of instruction and well-being. For the very salvation of primitive peoples Europeans had to absorb these differences—that is, this backwardness—into Western universality.

But once anthropologists discovered the complexity of the
traditions and rules governing the life of so-called primitive

societies (thanks in part to opportunities created by colonial expansion itself), they, as Lévi-Strauss has attested, switched gears. After indulging the vanity of Europeans for years, anthropologists began nurturing their guilty conscience instead. Savage, barbarian, primitive, these hateful and conde-scending terms had lost their intellectual validity. With these clichés fell the idea of a linear evolution of human beings and the distinction between backward and advanced peoples. In other words, the more the West affirmed itself as a world power, the more its anthropologists doubted the legitimacy of this domination. And at the moment UNESCO proposed to open a new chapter in the history of humanity, Lévi-Strauss reminded its founders, in the name of his discipline, that the era just ending was marked by colonialism as well as by war: by the arrogance of the West denying other possible forms of humanity as well as by the affirmation of the Nazis of a nat-ural hierarchy among people; by a power-hungry fascination with progress as well as by a crazed involvement with biology. What is more, Lévi-Strauss saw no distinction between attributing differences in cultures to nature and ascribing them to general developmental stages of knowledge, freedom, and technologies. As far as he was concerned, it was all the same thing; the same kind of *ethnocentrism* was at work in the two cases: That which is not me—inferior race or old-fash-ioned form on the social evolutionary scale —is not as good as me. To put an end to this infatuation with the white man once and for all, we had to complete the critique of race by calling into question the idea of civilization. People were not the same everywhere, nor were they easily divided into groups identifiable by sets of hereditary traits. There was human diversity, but it was not racial; there was civilization, but it was not unique. Anthropology, therefore, spoke of *cultures* in the plural, by which it meant

particular ways of life that were not transmitted, that could be understood only through concrete products—skills, customs, institutions, beliefs—rather than by potential capacities. Cultures corresponded to observable *values* instead of *truths* or what were supposed to be truths.[7]

Enlighten humanity to avoid the risk of falling back into barbarism: Lévi-Strauss endorsed the solemn goal of the founders of UNESCO but turned against the philosophy that inspired it. Testifying at the trial against barbarism, he identified the Enlightenment with the defense and not with the prosecution, in contrast to what Léon Blum and Clement Attlee had done so naturally before him.

The objective remained the same: destroy prejudice. But to achieve this goal it was no longer a matter of opening others to reason, but of opening ourselves to the reason of others. We would conquer ignorance, Lévi-Strauss argued, if we stopped trying to extend our culture to the rest of the world and accepted the idea that universalism was dead. In other words, we, the so-called civilized ones, should come down from our imaginary heights and recognize with humble clarity that we were only another kind of native. For the real enemy, obscurantism, was the blind rejection of that which is not ours,[8] not the resistance of others to our values and our way of seeing.

According to Condorcet Evil came from dividing human beings into two groups: those who believe and those who reason. For Lévi-Strauss all people reasoned, whether they practiced *la pensée sauvage* or scholarly thought, barbaric wisdom or *Logos*; whether they tinkered about with ideas (*bricolage*) or had formalized ways of thinking. The most gullible or wicked were those who thought they had exclusive rights to reason. Barbarian was not the opposite of civilized, "it is man who believes in barbarism in the first place."[9] And the Enlightenment was guilty of planting this belief in the West and of assigning to Europe the outrageous mission of overseeing the moral and intellectual development of all the peoples of the world.

The Second Death of Man

Lévi-Strauss created a school of thought. Adopting the ideas of structural anthropology, scholars in other fields in the social sciences went about the job of chasing ethnocentrism out of their disciplines. First in line were the historians. In an attempt to purge the present of all cultural imperialism, historians stopped unraveling the thread of time. They cut it instead, teaching us in the process *not* to seek in our ancestors a portrait of ourselves. Challenging their traditional role of giving us back our memory, they began to take the past apart before our very eyes, pointing out the places where we had broken with history. In the forceful words of Michel Foucault, they worked to "break into pieces everything which permitted the consoling game of recognition."[10] "Everything," that is, the permanence of the being as well as the becoming of the spirit, the stability of human nature and the linear outline of an ongoing process, continuously developing and maturing over time. Thus historical knowledge began to focus on subjects seemingly constant such as sexuality, feelings, family life, ways of being, eating, dying—and to expose their irreducible differences. It revealed a wide range of customs in aspects of culture where we anticipated finding no variation. A kaleidoscope of choices came into view in place of the linear process we identified with history. Realities we took as natural became historical objects, but, even more important, chronology itself no longer had any relation to progress. In other words, historians spread out all the disparate threads of the human adventure instead of tying them together in a single evolutionary line. And by focusing on the discontinuities, by refusing to see the past, present, and future as going in the same direction, by insisting on this essential *disorientation of history*, they sought to do with time what anthropologists were doing with space: to refute once and for all the naive and egocentric idea that man escapes completely into only one of the historical and geographic modes of his being. While some refused to place contemporary cultures on a hierarchical scale, others attacked false assumptions about the continuity of human time.

This confrontation with earlier periods reinforced the undermining effects of the research going on among peoples in the distant Amazon. The king had no clothes: we others, Europeans of the second half of the twentieth century, did not represent civilization. We were just one more culture, another variety of human being, as passing and perishable as the rest.

And this culture, sociologists quickly made clear, was multiple. Influenced by the struggle against colonialism, the most important and daring sociologists of the sixties combined Marxism with anthropology. Modern society, they proclaimed, was divided into classes, and each class was endowed with a distinct symbolic universe. Like Marx, they spoke of the class struggle, but inspired as they were by Lévi-Strauss, they went one step further, and attributed to each class a unique cultural or symbolic system:

The selection of meanings which objectively defines a group's or class's culture as a symbolic system, is arbitrary insofar as the structure and functions of that culture cannot be deduced from any universal principle, whether physical, biological or spiritual, not being linked by any sort of internal relation to the "nature of things" or any "human nature."[11]

It is true that among all these cultures only one was recognized as legitimate. But beware, sociologists warned us, of what seems obvious. The culture of the dominant class reigned, not by virtue of the intrinsic superiority of its products or values, but by the specific place it held in society. What the dominated classes suffered was similar to the humiliation of people colonized by the great European powers, both in moral and material terms. Their traditions were uprooted, their knowledge and tastes ridiculed, everything that gave substance and meaning to the experiences of people—"knowledge of the changing winds, of the land rich in secret signs, of organic matter easily understood, of the female cat that senses the coming of cold weather"[12]—were eliminated, without pity, from the legitimate culture. The aim was to ensure the universal communication of knowledge and to bring Enlightenment to those left behind in the dark. A lovely project, perhaps, but one that covered up, sociologists told us, a far less attractive enterprise involving two separate steps: first the *uprooting* of people, tearing them away from the web of customs and attitudes that constituted their collective identity; next the training or breaking them in, inculcating them with the dominant values, which had been promoted with dignity to represent the ideal culture or system of meanings. To cultivate the common people was to strip them of their authentic being and dress them up in a borrowed identity, the way colonialists clothed the tribes of Africa in the garb of ancestral Gaul. And this "symbolic violence" occurred in the very place established by Enlightenment philosophers as the perfect context for liberating men: the school.

To give one example, in the abundance of verbiage produced by our society, a few bits of ramblings earned the admiration of everyone and gained recognition as worthy of being taught. We called them literary products. Why these and not others? Because they had specific characteristics, a palpable superiority, understood by all, a kind of beauty that necessarily elevated them above ordinary speech? Structuralists challenged these assumptions. They discovered (or so they believed) that all narratives—whether stamped with the seal of "literature" or not—

belonged to the same system and obeyed the same rules. Under the egalitarian eye of science hierarchies were abolished and criteria used for making distinctions dismissed as arbitrary. No barrier separated masterpieces from the run-of-the-mill anymore. The same basic structure, the same general and elementary characteristics found in "great" novels (the excellence of which would henceforth be demystified with quotation marks) appeared in common forms of storytelling as well. That was what anthropology taught: "Human societies, like individuals,—in their games, dreams or moments of madness—never create in the absolute sense, but are limited to the choice of certain combinations from an ideal repertoire which we could reconstruct."[13] Two myths, two dreams, two moments of madness or confession were never exactly alike, but that did not give us the right to make value judgments. They were only variations of the same activity of combination. What conclusion should we draw? The definition of art was "at stake in the class struggle."[14] If a particular text was venerated and made an object of study, that was because the dominant group could use it to prescribe its vision of the world for everyone in society. There was violence at the root of any process of evaluation.

And so, in their analysis of European society, sociologists transferred the scenario anthropologists had perfected to describe the relationship of the West to peoples of other traditions. In both cases, in effect, ethnocentrism acted ruthlessly: the "reign of the culturally arbitrary" claimed a monopoly on legitimacy, devaluing the art of living and ways of thinking of others, casting off the unfamiliar into the shadows of savagery or ignorance.

We all know that humanism came into being with the dis-covery of the New World. Contact with exotic peoples opened up the religious citadel to the possibility of comparison, ruin-ing, little by little, the authority of the Revelation. Going beyond their own borders, seeing, "from one day to the next a new cult, different manners and ceremonies," as La Bruyère put it in his chapter in *Les Esprits forts*, Europeans saw that their own beliefs were relative. Man could stand on his own: act, think, distinguish between good and evil, without the guiding light of faith. Free of God, the thinking subject became the foundation of the world, the source of all values.

In the twentieth century with the rediscovery of preliterate societies, it was no longer God but man himself who was open to question. Anthropologists, in effect, denounced the double lie of human progress and human immutability. Before anthropol-ogists made travel a serious enterprise, Europeans abroad merely projected their dreams, their arrogance, and rational thought onto other peoples of the world. When they were not looking down on these people for being backward, they turned them into noble savages. Either way, they stripped them of who they were and used them to serve a mythic function: to make West-ern culture *natural*. By saying, "*I am Man*," they could, in all good conscience, devour the rest of the world. If we now wanted the leviathan of the West to regurgitate what it had swallowed, we had to do more than grant *independence* to subjugated peoples. We had to pronounce that all cultures were *equal*.

And there were two ways of bringing this about: some tried to show that all human beings, despite the multiplicity of cultures, shared the same unconscious, timeless, and anonymous logic: "The forms are basically the same for all minds, ancient or modern, primitive or civilized."[15] Others, more extreme in their position, rejected the idea of a common logic and argued, with Michel Foucault, for "the absolute divergence"[16] of systems of thought and social practices. In both cases man died as an independent subject, becoming instead the field of action for forces or structures that had escaped consciousness. As Foucault aptly put it, "Where 'it speaks,' man no longer exists."[17] Thus, a revolution in thought accompanied the political work of decolonization: man—this "unitary concept of universal significance"[18]—gave way to diversity, absent of any hierarchy of cultural personalities.

This was not the first time that such a revolution took place. Spengler praised himself for causing a similar rebellion. Before him, we remember, Herder blamed Voltaire and his followers for seeing their values as beacons of light, and then, using the pretext that they offered enlightenment, for trying to make the world's peoples the same. Opposing the idea of man—this hypostasis of the Frenchman—Herder had already introduced the notion of the inexhaustible diversity of people in all their unique possibilities. Now once again those professing *the philosophy of decolonization* evoked the ideas of German Romanticism. Denouncing the basic inhumanity of humanism and looking for the particular, the historic, the regional behind everything that might be mistaken for universal, they found themselves staging an old play, changing the characters and scenery only slightly. In the new version the West took the role France once played all

by itself, and the action expanded to consider the relation
Europe had with the rest of the world as well as with the diverse
members of its own society. Despite these changes the drama
remained essentially the same: the conflict between those who
saw man in the singular and those who saw him in the plural.
Thus the philosophy of decolonization fought ethnocentrism
with the arguments and concepts molded by the German
romantics in their struggle against the Enlightenment.

Let us be clear: this return to a romantic notion of culture was
inspired by a desire to atone for past sins, not by the sudden
awakening of tribal pride. Like Herder, contemporary antihu-
manists showed that man was not only a beautiful ideal but a useful fiction, a convenient pretext provided by a particular civilization eager to impose its law. Again, like Herder, they chased out
from under the metaphysical spirit celebrated by Enlightenment
thought an eminently concrete being. The subject elevated by
the West to a place beyond time and space actually had a body,
an identity, a history. And finally, like Herder, they believed that

men do not act as members of a group by following the way each
one feels as an individual: each man feels according to the way he is
permitted or prescribed to act. Customs exist as external norms
before they become internal feelings and these norms without feelings determine the feelings individuals have as well as the circumstances in which they may or must express them.[19]

But Herder was speaking before everything else for his own
people, whereas the philosophers of decolonization *were speak-*

ing for the Other. Settling matters with their own tradition, they tried to do away with the illusion Europeans had delighted in for so long, that their culture had no equal. Instead of the collective me, without hesitation they took the side of the non-me, of the proscribed, the excluded, the outsider. Wanting to rehabilitate the foreigner, they abolished any sense of commonality among people. If they insisted on what made them different, they did so in order to return to other cultures the dignity stolen from them through the exploits of Western imperialism. If they made a list of all these differences, they did so because they wanted to make up for the wrongs of their own civilization, to weaken the desire for power in the society that saw them be born, and to cure philosophy of the tendency always to translate the other into its own language. If they exalted the multiplicity of particular ways of reasoning, it was to make their own more open and modest before the ideas of others. Xenophiles, they embraced the cause of the humble and disinherited, decreeing the death of abstract Man in the name of individual people, with all their differences. Thus they attacked ethnic nationalism with the same vigor as Julien Benda in *The Treason of the Intellectuals,* but they drew the opposite conclusion: down with universal values.

A Portrait of the Decolonized World

The philosophy of decolonization has, without doubt, helped third world peoples emancipate themselves from a system of values that justified their subjugation in the first place. Having internalized the perspective of the colonizer, the elites of Africa and Asia used to protect themselves from feeling alienated by accepting the idea that all cultures were the same and that the value of each revealed itself from within its own context. But once the social sciences provided criteria other than technology for determining a people's level of advancement, the earlier explanation for Europe's superiority fell apart, allowing its victims to see that the West was not so fascinating. "Kilometers of roads, canals, and railway tracks . . . tons of cotton or cacao exported, hectars of olive trees or vineyards planted . . . diseases cured, the standard of living raised far above what it had been"[20]—these statistical arguments, usually invoked to justify colonialism, lost their power to intimidate at the same time superficial assumptions about the psychology of natives smashed into smithereens. Customs previously scorned by simplistic ideas about progress assumed legitimacy once again; an entire past, obscured or disqualified from history, came out from under the shadows where the West, committed to ideas about the forward march of time, felt justified in placing it; "millions of men torn away from their gods, their land, their customs, their way of living, from life itself, from dance and wisdom"[21] regained possession of themselves: they were no longer savages or barbarians waiting for salvation but the inheritors of venerable traditions.

With the support of the philosophy of decolonization, the concept of culture, the symbol of the imperialist West, broke away, moving over to represent the very societies it had previously nurtured with condescending attention. The theme of cultural identity permitted the colonized to stop being mimics, allowing them to replace their degrading parody of the invader with the affirmation of their cultural difference, to turn into a subject of pride what they had been taught to be ashamed of. This very idea, however, took away any distance they had before their own community. They could not claim to be on the outside, to avoid the demands of their culture. Nor could they step back from their traditions, for they had struggled to deliver themselves from that very misfortune by shaking off the yoke of colonialism. For them to achieve independence was to recover their culture. It was logical that the majority of new states born out of these circumstances wanted to make their own traditions part of their national life: to bind individuals tightly to the collectivity, to cement the unity of the nation. To guarantee without any sign of weakness the integrity and cohesion of society. To make sure in the name of culture that no zealous critique disturbed the *cult of time-honored beliefs*. To assure, in sum, the absolute triumph of the socially minded spirit over any other.

As Hélé Béji showed in *Désenchantement national*—an admirable if little-known book—cultural identity was a means of resistance under colonial rule but became an instrument of repression after the Europeans left: "When it is a matter of defending myself against the physical presence of the invader, the force of my identity dazzles and reassures me. But once my identity takes the place of this invader or rather my own (national) effigy sets itself up as the authority and surrounds me, in all logic I should not have the right to challenge it."[22] People could not rebel against themselves: those benefiting from independence found themselves closed in by the restrictions imposed by the unanimity of sentiment that followed immediately after the liberation from foreign rule. Left to themselves, the formerly colonized became their own captives, stuck in a collective identity that had freed them from the tyranny of European values. No sooner had they said, "We won," than they lost the right to express themselves in anything but the first-person plural. We: the pronoun of authenticity recovered, of obligatory homogeneity. This pronoun evoked the warm feeling of a fraternity of soldiers, proclaiming grammatically that colonial rule weathered badly, that it had frozen and cracked. This was the birth of a community unto itself, the end of a period when members of the same nation could fight among themselves. This was the call to revolt, the soliloquy of power. If there was no place for the collective subject in the logic of colonialism, there was no place for the individual in the logic of identity politics.

In translating the idea of cultural identity into political terms, the most fitting form of government turned out to be one-party rule. If we did not see freedoms flourish with the independence of the colonies, but greater conformity, bureaucracy, and the rise of single-party systems, we must look for explanations in the very values expressed by anticolonial struggles and not at the betrayal of local bourgeoisies or the subversion of newly won rights in the interest of European powers. The transition from the impassioned revolutionary to the cold bureaucrat took place all by itself, without the intervention of a malevolent third party. What is more, the national disenchantment so lucidly described by Hélé Béji derived from the idea of the nation that prevailed during the struggle against Western imperialism.

To be convinced one need only reread *The Wretched of the Earth*. Written during the impassioned years of the insurrection, Frantz Fanon placed individualism at the top of the list of enemy values:

The native intellectual had learned from his masters that the individual ought to express himself fully. The colonialist bourgeoisie had hammered into the native's mind the idea of a society of individuals where each person shuts himself up in his own subjectivity, and whose only wealth is individual thought. Now the native who has the opportunity to return to the people during the struggle for freedom will discover the falseness of this theory.[23]

Separated from each other by their oppressor, atomized, condemned to endure the egoism of "everyone for himself," during the war everything changed. While fighting, the colonized experienced the ecstatic feeling of being one with each other. The sick and illusory world of dispersed wills gave way to total unity. Instead of tending stubbornly toward self-affirmation or cultivating their specificities in a sterile way, people immersed themselves in the "popular tide." Instead of expressing their own ideas, they returned to the bosom of their community. The individual, a false reality, was abolished: everyone was like everybody else, the bearer of the same identity; the mystical body of the nation had absorbed each and every soul.

Thus, once the war was over and sovereignty achieved, what incentive was there to reinstate the individual? Throughout the struggle for liberation the new nations called the very idea a pathology. For what miraculous reason would they now turn around and make the individual a positive principle after the victory? How could this organic whole, this indivisible unity—celebrated during combat—be transformed into an association of autonomous people once they all lay down their arms? A nation whose primary goal was to wipe out the individuality of its citizens could not become a state committed to protecting their rights as individuals.

Although Frantz Fanon made it his mission to renounce Europe—and he did so with a passion—he ended up taking sides in a debate about the nation that had divided Europe since the French Revolution. Favoring the Volk over a society of individuals, he sought to replace colonial rule with the national spirit, with "the affirmation of an original idea propounded as an absolute."[24] He may have been able to "vomit up"[25] the oppressor's culture. He may have enthusiastically recommended that the colonized "pull out his knife or at least make sure it is within reach"[26] when confronted with Western values, but his book still subscribes expressly to one line of *European nationalism*. And the majority of movements for national liberation followed suit. With Fanon as their prophet, the movement chose the ethnic theory of the nation over the elective theory, preferring cultural identity—the modern translation of Volksgeist—to "the daily plebiscite" or to the idea of "long-term *association*." If these movements of liberation ended up as regimes of oppression over and over again, this was because they, in the tradition of political romanticism, based relations among humans on the mystical model of fusion rather than on the legal model of the contract. They conceived of freedom as a collective attribute, never as an individual possession.

At first, it is true, most of the new states sought to combine cultural restoration with revolutionary ambitions. While aggressively nationalistic, they also saw themselves as the new *Internationale* of the exploited. Drawing on the analyses of anthropology and the class struggle, they demanded recognition both as nations with distinct cultures and as nations of the proletariat. Aspiring to find their roots, they also sought ways to hasten the birth of the new man. On the one hand they challenged universalism in the name of cultural diversity, on the other they defended it in the name of revolution. In other words, without realizing it postcolonial states had synthesized the positions of de Maistre and Marx. Following de Maistre, they proclaimed: "Man does not exist; there is no cultural paradigm common to all humanity; different national traditions each have their own reality (and set of values)." But agreeing with Marx, they added: "Man does not exist *yet*; and it was incumbent on the wretched of the earth to make him happen."

Marx himself would no doubt be offended by this unnatural marriage of his ideas with nationalism. For the author of the *Communist Manifesto* it was clearly understood: the proletariat had no country. "The nationality of the worker," he wrote, for example, "is neither French, nor English, nor German; it is *labor*, *free slavery, self-huckstering.* His government is neither French, nor English, nor German; it is *capital.* The air he breathes is neither French, nor English, nor German; it is *factory air.*[27] To those who inherited the Enlightenment, who believed they could organize nations on the basis of *contract,* Marx responded by saying that every society was governed by the *conflict* between the bourgeoisie and the working class. To the romantics who wanted to revive the national spirit, he replied that the bourgeoisie, with unlimited cynicism, had dissolved age-old attachments, broken up traditional loyalties, wiped out the unique character of different nations. The social contract had been replaced with the division of classes, cultural diversity with the world market and universal interdependence. For Marx the nation was doomed; it mattered little whether one defined it as an ethnic community or the will of individuals. But his writing waxed eloquent, with lyrical fervor, every time he spoke of the world uniting and of provincial ideas disappearing.

Since his prediction for Europe was systematically proved wrong in the second half of the nineteenth century, Marx's successors had to consider the national question once again. After lengthy debates among Austro-Hungarian Marxists, Bundists, Bolsheviks, and Luxembourgists, Joseph Stalin's definition in 1913 carried the day: "The nation is a human community, stable, historically constituted, born out of a commonality of language, territory, economic life and psychological conditioning, all of which translates into a cultural community."[28]

Nations are stubborn, and Stalin accepted the persistence of this historical phenomenon. But his doctrinal conversion did not go so far as to repudiate basic theoretical premises. If there had to be nations, he preferred to integrate the ethnic concept into the body of revolutionary thought than the elective one. For when push came to shove, he could admit that besides being economically determined, men were also conditioned by their language, territory, and culture. But entirely inadmissible was the idea that membership to a particular nation might be the result of reasoned deliberation or free choice. Such a theory would clearly contradict the fundamental principle of historical materialism: "It is not consciousness which determines life; but life which determines consciousness."[29]

The marriage of Marxism to political romanticism is in the process of breaking up, after many happy years of union, stretching from the dawn of the Russian Revolution to the struggles against colonialism, when non-European cultures finally gained recognition. Since Soviet imperialism proved at least as voracious as Western imperialism, third world states and those liberation movements still in existence began rejecting socialist ideology in favor, exclusively, of the Volksgeist. Cultural identity justified itself: fundamentalism swept away progressive phrases, and the invocation of the collectivity no longer made reference to the revolution of the international proletariat.

Communism was experiencing an irreversible decline, but what died along with it was not totalitarian thinking but the idea of a world common to all people. Marx had definitely lost, but to Joseph de Maistre. We should therefore not be surprised if, as Octavio Paz has written, "in what we call the third world, there reigns a Caligula with a thousand faces, bearing different names and appearing in many guises."[30]

Of the two European models of the nation, the third world opted en masse for the worse one, and they did so with the enthusiastic blessings of Western intellectuals. To give substance to their deep respect for humanity, anthropology and all the other social sciences took it upon themselves to criticize the spirit of the Enlightenment. As early as 1947 the American Anthropological Association submitted to the United Nations a draft for the Declaration of the Rights of Man that would cure the great humanitarian principles of their tendency toward formalism and abstraction, and of their ineffectuality. The first article read as follows: "The individual realizes his personality through his culture, hence respect for individual differences entails a respect for cultural differences."[31] The impulse, though generous, was about as clumsy as that of a bear stepping on the face of the sleeping gardener in its attempt to chase away a fly. At the very moment the Other got his culture back, he lost his freedom: his personal name disappeared into the name of the community; he became an example, nothing more than an interchangeable representative of a particular class of beings. While receiving an unconditional welcome, the Other found he no longer had any freedom of movement, any means of escape. All originality was taken away from him; he was trapped insidiously in his difference. Those who thought they had left behind the idea of abstract man in order to embrace the real human being, had, in effect, done away with the space that existed between the individuals and the collectivities from which they came, a space that anthropologists in the Enlightenment period had insisted upon preserving. Under the guise of altruism they turned the Other into a homogeneous bloc, destroying the individual realities of others. Out of love for the Other they deprived the former colonies of experiencing European democracy.

Race and Culture

Those adhering to the politics of cultural identity had two bêtes noires: individualism and cosmopolitanism. Turning once again to Frantz Fanon:

This traditional weakness, which is almost congenital to the national consciousness of underdeveloped countries, is not solely the result of the mutilation of the colonized people by the colonial régime. It is also the result of the intellectual laziness of the national middle class, of its spiritual penury, and *of the profoundly cosmopolitan mold of its mind set.*[32]

Independence settled nothing. With the threat of internal disintegration loomed the possibility of foreign elements sneaking back in. Having only just left the state of limbo, the new nation had to struggle constantly on two fronts: to blend the opinions of many into the will of one and to protect its specific culture from any form of corruption. "Everything foreign, everything introduced for no good reason to the life of a people, leads to illness and must be removed to maintain the health of [the group],"[33] the German romantics had already said. In the same spirit those espousing the politics of cultural identity called for the elimination of colonial arrogance by evoking frightening images of mixing, obsessions with purity, and the specter of contamination.

Leaning back on the universality of his civilization, the white man had placed himself in the center of history, expressing contempt for archaic peoples whom he saw as vegetating in their difference. Delighted to have won back their difference, third world nationalists defended their particularism from the corruption of outside influences: they rejected the foreigner because he was other, not because he was backward. Putting it crudely, they replaced the old colonial form of racism, based on inequalities, with a racism based on difference.

The term *racism* itself is deceptive. It brings together two perspectives whose genesis, logic, and motivations are entirely unrelated. On the one hand racism measures all the nations of the world by the same scale of values, on the other it proclaims there is no basis for comparison. On the one hand it ranks every group within a single system, on the other it destroys any possibility of seeing unity within the human species. On the one hand it sees differences as inferior, on the other it affirms the absolute, impenetrable, untranslatable character of distinct ways of being. On the one hand it classifies within a single system, on the other it divides everything up. From the perspective of one, you cannot be a Persian, from the perspective of the other you cannot be a man, for there is no common measure of humanity between the Persian and the European. One declares that civilization is one, the other that ethnic groups are multiple and incomparable. And if one point of view leads to colonialism, the other culminates in Hitler.[34]

We can now see more clearly the fundamental defect in the philosophy of decolonization: it confused two distinct historical phenomena. Turning Nazism into a variety of Western racism, developed for domestic purposes, the proponents of the philosophy of decolonization saw nothing more in this episode than Europe applying to itself "colonialist procedures which, until then, had been reserved exclusively for the Arabs of Algeria, the coolies of India and the Negroes [*nègres*] of Africa."[35] As a result they ended up fighting the evils of ethnocentrism with the weapons of the Volksgeist, meekly supporting Frantz Fanon as he said: "Truth . . . is all that protects the natives and ruins the foreigners,"[36] even though, by speaking in this way, the author of *The Wretched of the Earth* had repeated, almost verbatim, the attack Barrès made on abstract justice and on absolute truth. We read, for example, in *Les Déracinés*: "Truth is what satisfies the needs of our soul." And in *Mes Cahiers*: "It is necessary to teach French truth, that is to say, what is most useful to the nation."[37]

It is true that, with the convergence of work done in the social and natural sciences, the concept of race has lost favor. Explanations based in nature for differences among human groups would immediately be rejected by contemporary scholarship. The irrefutable discoveries of biology and anthropology make it impossible to maintain that by virtue of genetic heredity the human species is divided into clearly defined ethnic groups, each provided with its own transmissible way of thinking. We have learned to distinguish between the innate and the acquired and no longer attribute to our biological heritage what belongs, in fact, to our history or tradition. A decisive sign of our intellectual and moral progress, we now know the relative and transitory nature of traits once regarded as eternal facts of humanity. In sum, the biological argument is no longer relevant. Everything is cultural: from religious rituals to industrial technology, from food to styles of dress, from literature to team sports.

The fact is, however, those who invented the idea of the national spirit knew this as well. They were the first to reject human nature, replacing the concept with the irreducible variety of cultures. It was they who transformed the immutable world of the philosophers into a shimmering landscape of collective entities, standing side by side. The theory of races that came later on *naturalized this rejection of human nature* and, more generally, everything else that might transcend the diversity of cultures. For the proponents of a racial theory the specific traits of each people were engraved in the genes; the national "spirits" became quasi species endowed with a hereditary character, permanent and indelible.

We believe we have since discredited the concept of race, but have we really made any progress? Like the racists before them, contemporary fanatics of cultural identity confine individuals to their group of origin. Like them, they carry differences to the absolute extreme, and in the name of the multiplicity of specific causalities destroy any possibility of a natural or cultural community among peoples.

When Renan maintained, "Man belongs neither to his language nor his race; he belongs only to himself, for he is a free being, that is to say, a moral being," Barrès responded, "To be moral is *not to wish to be free from one's race*."[38] Do we really believe that to refute Barrès all we have to do is to translate his biological ravings into the language of cultural difference and proclaim: to be moral is to want not to be free from one's culture and to oppose, by whatever means necessary, the influence of foreigners? To do so, on the contrary, we perpetuate the cult of the collective soul, of which the discourse on biological race was a temporary and frenzied version, prolonging a cult that appeared with the idea of the Volksgeist. In replacing the biological argument with a cultural one, racism has not been wiped out, it has simply been returned to its point of departure, to square one.

UNESCO'S Double-talk

In 1971, twenty years after the publication of *Race and History*, UNESCO invited Claude Lévi-Strauss to give the keynote address at the ceremonies marking the beginning of the International Year of the Struggle Against Racism. Everyone assumed the illustrious anthropologist would demonstrate once again that there was no scientific basis for the concept of race. Contrary to expectations, Lévi-Strauss chose to take the word *race* seriously and return to the old question of the relationship between race and culture. With the help of the more recent work in population genetics, he provided a solution to this problem diametrically opposed to the one offered by European scholars of the nineteenth and early twentieth centuries:

The cultural forms adopted in various places by human beings, their ways of life in the past or in the present, determine to a very great extent the rhythm of their biological evolution and its direction. Far from having to ask whether or not culture is a function of race, we are discovering that race—or what is generally meant by this term, is one function, among others, of culture.[39]

Even though Lévi-Strauss had reversed the relationship between race and culture, his assertion created a scandal, shocking those who had come to hear him. The author of *Race and History*, who had, in a way, drafted the second constitutive act of UNESCO, was now accused of heresy. His crime? Returning some legitimacy to the concept of race, "let[ting] the wolf back into the fold."[40] We might smile at the zealotry of an institution whose opposition to racist thought went so far as to dismiss, a priori, any thinking that took race seriously—of an institution that called on science to come to the rescue, only to reject the research of those whose findings challenged accepted dogma. But irony on our part is not quite enough. As the word *race* became taboo at UNESCO, those committed to typological thinking and the fetishism of difference reassembled themselves under the irreproachable banner of culture. Now, in current resolutions of the organization, we read that human beings draw the substance of who they are from the group to which they belong. A person's own individual identity blends in with the identity of the collectivity.[41] Everything—beliefs, values, intelligence, or feelings—comes from a complex of factors: climate, lifestyle, language; from those elements making up what we used to call Volksgeist and call culture today. The integrity of the group is important, we are told, not the autonomy of individuals. Thus education no longer seeks to provide students with the tools to choose among the many beliefs, opinions, and customs that make up their heritage, but to plunge them instead into this ocean of traditions, *head first*:

Far from constituting two parallel fields, culture and education were intimately intermingled and should be developed symbiotically, so that culture could infuse and nourish education, which was by far the best means of transmitting culture and consequently of promoting or strengthening cultural identity.[42]

Having drawn the conclusion from the Nazi episode that there was a connection between the absence of free thought and the rise of barbarism, the founders of UNESCO had wanted to create an instrument on an international scale for transmitting culture to the majority of the people of the world. Their successors used the same vocabulary, but they attributed to these words an entirely different meaning. Although they continued to stress the importance of culture and education, they no longer saw culture as something acquired (as Bildung), but given at birth. Using this new insight, they reversed the educational process: where once there was "I," now there was "We." Instead of having to cultivate myself (thereby getting out of my own little world), now I have to rediscover my culture, defined as "the whole range of knowledge and values which were not specifically taught but which every member of a community nevertheless knows."[43] This is what Enlightenment thought called lack of education or prejudice, the celebration of which Lichtenberg was already predicting two hundred years ago: "Today, we seek to spread knowledge everywhere, but who knows whether in a few centuries there will not be universities dedicated to reestablishing our former ignorance?"

Keeping Lichtenberg in mind, we now see delegates to the twentieth session of the General Conference of UNESCO adopting "by acclamation" a "declaration concerning the contribution of the mass media to strengthening peace and international understanding, to the promotion of human rights and to countering racism, apartheid and incitement to war."[44] The delegates voted to establish a New World Order of Information and Communication to counterbalance the power of the four major press agencies in the West—U.P.I., Associated Press, Reuters, and A.F.P. (Agence France-Presse)—by developing and recognizing third world agencies and media. "The establishment of a new balance and a better exchange of information" should allow the world to hear "the voices . . . of oppressed peoples" (article II), "the views and aspirations of the younger generation" (article IV), "the points of view presented by those who consider that the information published and disseminated about them has seriously prejudiced opinion about their efforts to strengthen peace and international understanding, to promote human rights, or to combat racism, apartheid, and incitement to war" (article V).[45]

The authors of the New World Order of Information and Communication accused the four major press agencies of having a monopoly on the free circulation of news, of stifling that freedom with their monopoly, and of imposing a single direction on the flow of information among people. According to them, before being an individual a journalist from the West was a Westerner. His origins determined what he said. No matter how hard he might try to wipe the slate clean of preconceived notions and open himself up to the world around him, he was forced to look at things a certain way, his culture would never leave his side: wherever he went, his culture went with him. Although he might think he was interpreting, studying, or even simply describing events taking place in another society, he was, in fact, reflecting the prejudices of his own. He might think he was free and able to see things objectively, but he remained conditioned by the particular values of his own mental universe. When the journalist did not directly serve the interests of the West, he still yielded to the impulses of his cultural identity. Put another way, at worst he was an agent, at best a symptom, but, either way, an emissary of the West. In order to defend freedom of information, it was necessary, therefore, to prevent prejudicial reporting. And there were two ways of doing this: either by protecting people from propaganda or by challenging the voice of the West with the voices of the rest of the world, expressing faithfully in their name the "aspirations" of their culture. In clear language this meant abdicating all personal initiatives and originality.

Whether they were talking about the New World Order of Information and Communication or the politics of education, members of UNESCO justified social control and distrust of foreigners in cultural terms. Under the unchanging banner of an indisputable word, nobody even noticed when UNESCO began spreading values that the original mandate of the organization called for combating. And the more the antiracism of today resembled the racism of yesterday, the more the word *race* became sacrilegious. Given the turn of events, we can now see why Lévi-Strauss, who inspired the great transformation that changed culture into identity, provoked indignation without altering his argument virtually at all.

But Lévi-Strauss also caused a scandal because he refused in his talk to recognize as racist "the attitude of individuals or groups whose loyalty to certain values make them partially or entirely unreceptive to other values."[46] To members of UNESCO, devoted to the organization's founding mission of promoting harmony and fraternity among peoples, this measured rehabilitation of some forms of intolerance was judged, quite simply, intolerable. For in contrast to the "barbarous preaching of national particularisms"[47] of earlier times, which turned into hateful speeches and open celebrations of war, the present-day declarations of UNESCO were resolutely idyllic. They spoke only of peace, understanding, and love.

Still, to turn on Lévi-Strauss in this fashion was no small achievement. By what kind of magic did people expect that individuals locked into their own cultures would feel a spontaneous passion for customs or ways of thinking quite foreign to their own traditions? If the richness of humanity consisted entirely in the multiplicity of their different modes of existence, if "the honor of having created aesthetic and spiritual values which gave meaning to life" had become once again the "old particularisms," as Lévi-Strauss had suggested and those professing the faith of UNESCO had alluded to as well, then feelings of mutual hostility among cultures were not only normal but indispensable. They represented "the price to be paid so that the value systems of each spiritual family or community might preserve and find within itself the resources necessary for renewal."[48]

From the perspective of those supporting the philosophy of colonialism—at UNESCO and elsewhere—Lévi-Strauss had made a mistake in calling things by their proper name and associating his ideas about culture with measured praise for the intolerance of others. They preferred not to follow the anthropologist to the logical conclusion of his position. As a result anticipation of war gave way to a limp and moralizing celebration of universal understanding, one in which people worshipped the cult of difference and excluded universalism, eliminated the individual in the name of freedom, and evoked a spirit in which the word *culture* served as a humanist standard for dividing humanity into insuperable and irreducible collective entities.

PART THREE

TOWARD A MULTICULTURAL SOCIETY?

The Disappearance of the Dreyfusards

To each people their own cultural personality; to each culture its own moral values, traditions, and rules of conduct. Third world activists, struggling against the supremacy of the West, are no longer the only ones expressing this point of view. Those who oppose the "invasion" of Europe by inhabitants of the developing nations have asserted the same in recent years. For the *new right* (to use the staggering term given to this ideological movement when it appeared on the intellectual scene in the late 1970s) the natives are those who live on the Old Continent and the colonists the millions of people who, fulfilling the prophecy of Houari Boumediene, have left "the impoverished regions of the southern world, to pour into the relatively accessible parts of the Northern Hemisphere in search of their own survival." Famished colonists, true, but given their overwhelming numbers, they could swamp and depersonalize the peoples of Europe.

In contrast to doctrinaire supporters of colonial expansion, advocates of cultural identity do not exclude the Other from the category of people capable of thinking. They see them instead as representing another kind of humanity, as having their own unique way of being. These proponents of difference have no interest in the imperialist idea of stamping out diversity and spreading Western values, of disregarding the infinite variety of human traditions. What they want is to protect Europe from the

harmful ways of foreigners, to preserve Europe's cultural differences from the outside world. Loaded with ethnographic references, armed with quotations from the works of Lévi-Strauss,
Leach, Berque, and Jaulin, they propose the "general political
postulate that humanity exists in the plural."[1] Separated one from
the other by an insurmountable chasm, there is no one set of universal criteria to judge or rank the achievements of diverse peoples. Thus, they conclude, "It is a tragic mistake to want to have
communities representing different civilizations live together in
the same country. Confrontations are inevitable. The major con-
flicts are not about race, but about systems of belief and culture."[2]

Before denouncing this imposture, this caricature of third
world ideology turned back on itself, this racism without race,
we should not forget that anthropologists themselves borrowed
the concept of culture from the political romantics. As we have
already seen, it takes very little to reduce individual identity to
collective identity, to imprison people in their group of origin,
without ever calling on the laws of heredity. Those championing the cause of a European way of life were not being
opportunistic when they embraced the progressive slogan, "the
right to be different." In proclaiming equal dignity for all cultures, they did not appropriate the words of their enemies for
propagandistic purposes, they merely took what belonged to
themselves. Put another way, if any group acted deceitfully in
recognizing diversity, it was not the "new right," for they, unlike
the anti-imperialist left, represented a tradition long committed
to *making difference work.*

And now, after forty years of purgatory, the new right enjoys legitimacy enough to be able once again to convert mainstream conservatives to its point of view. With the rise of unemployment, immigrant workers from abroad, considered a godsend in better times, are now seen as a problem. Their presence gives new life to the mystique of the Volksgeist, first and foremost among those who previously opposed decolonization and celebrated the West's power to assimilate others, but who now defend the specificity of Europe. Sympathy for the Volksgeist has found its way into respectable political circles and has even influenced acts of government.[3]

Herder, in other words, is everywhere, representing both sides of the political spectrum. No longer silenced by post-World War II taboos, he reigns supreme, inspiring at the same time declarations glorifying a sacred sense of self and vehement denunciations of egocentricity. He has given voice to unyielding celebrations of ethnic identity and expressions of respect for foreigners, aggressive outbursts by xenophobes and generous pronouncements by xenophiles, chilly invitations to close in on oneself and encouragement to take the beautiful risk of opening up to others. Those favoring hospitality respond with indignation when they hear people shamelessly proclaim that the spirit of Europe is threatened with annihilation by the uprooted of the third world and that the only way to assure the harmonious development of diverse human communities is to separate them once again:

Since all cultural forms are of equal value, we do not have the right, we Frenchmen, we Europeans, to prefer our own. We cannot establish our own code of conduct as the norm for everyone. In recent years, as we became conscious of our own specificity, we cured ourselves of the tendency to dominate the world. Now, given the new context created by immigration, this very same act of self-awareness justifies transforming the universe familiar to us into a *multicultural* society.

Multicultural is the key word in the war against ethnic purity, the basic concept defending the pleasures and virtues of diversity over the monotony of a homogeneous landscape. But do not be deceived. Despite their sharp differences and tense relations, the two sides share the same position on relativism. They have conflicting credos but the same vision of the world. In both cases they see cultures as all-encompassing entities, distinctly different one from the other.

At the turn of the century, when supporters of Dreyfus challenged "French truth" and the *raison d'État*, they did so in the name of absolute norms and universal values. Today, as the philosophy used to condemn Dreyfus gains favor once again, the present opposition—numerous, determined, and furiously eloquent—defends its side by claiming that everything is cultural. There are, in other words, no Dreyfusards left.

For the sake of argument let us accept the position that the identity of each human group originates in its culture, using the word *culture* the way UNESCO defines the term: "The totality of knowledge and values never specifically taught, but which all members of the community know." Let us suppose, for example, as Régis Debray has suggested, that France is "a childhood memory . . . a refrain from a song, a nostalgic memory of fountains and foam, of waterfalls and potholes . . . of the way one deals with taxicab drivers, faucets, and waiters in a café, with the look girls give and with the passage of time."[4] A society operating in such a mechanistic way could never grant the wish expressed by the same Debray and become "a country without Jules, Hippolytes, and Ernests, but one with people called Boris, Ursula, Jamila, Rachel, Milan and Julio."[5] It is Hippolyte, not Jamila, who is French *through and through*, who was born in the wooded farmlands of Normandy or spent every summer with his family in Dordogne. It was generations of Ernests and Jules who gave Christophe, Adrien, and Grégoire—not Milan (Kundera) or Julio (Cortázar)—their typically cocky sense of humor, their shrewd, biting wit.

Barrès was more consistent. He knew that *the unconscious was uncompromising*; it could not be shared, exchanged, or acquired. That was why it became for him the locus of a people's national identity. When he said that one was French by birth, not by choice, it was to keep foreigners out. To put it another way, we must make a choice: we cannot celebrate universal communication at the same time we insist on the existence of nontransferable differences. After having attached the French to their country through ties of affective memory, we cannot populate France with peoples who have no access to this memory and have nothing in common with the other groups of immigrants except that they have all been excluded. We create an impossible contradiction in seeking to establish rules for welcoming diverse ethnic groups based on principles affirming the primacy of cultural roots.

A Pedagogy of Cultural Relativism

The spiritual itinerary claimed by Régis Debray has taken him from the socialist dream of internationalism to the inevitable reality of cultures. During the heroic times of guerrilla warfare, he participated in the great uprisings of subjugated peoples against the masters of the world. Without renouncing his revolutionary youth, he now sees that the moment for carrying the torch has passed. The former fellow traveler of Che Guevara claims today that man has roots, a genealogy, cultural memory; he is not defined by his interests or hopes alone. Before choosing to join a war (or a career), man has already been launched, in spite of himself, on a collective destiny. Before becoming educated or uneducated, bourgeois or working class, he is part of a culture, submerged, body and soul, in the immanence of his community.

And Debray knows from experience about the primacy of the archaic group over the individual. As a Frenchman he is master of himself in only an illusory way. His sense of individualism comes after his sense of belonging to the group, and cannot therefore dominate it: his "real self does not belong to him, but to his country."[6] Would Debray not want to subscribe to the beautiful declaration made by Montesquieu?

If I knew something that was useful to me, but would hurt my family, I would evict it from my thoughts. If I knew something useful to my family, but not to my nation, I would try to forget it. If I knew something useful to my country, but harmful to Europe and to the human species, I would consider it a crime.[7]

Such a profession of faith is the opposite of Debray's assertion that "group instinct places Europe before the human species, the nation before Europe, and the family before the nation."[8] And according to Debray man can do and say what he likes in an effort to eliminate clan morality, but universalistic declarations are only "luxurious abstractions."[9] In the end the cosmopolitan aristocrat succumbs to the peasant within him; the voice of instinct inevitably brings him back to the fold.

Régis Debray has not abandoned as such the ideal of brotherhood. He takes Barrès's side against the Enlightenment and then opposes Barrès's successors. Placing himself at the imaginary confluence of two incompatible traditions— France, the land of the Reign of Terror and France, the land of asylum—he subordinates ethical choices of individuals to the cultural reflexes of ethnic groups, editing out in the process any trace of hatred of foreigners. In the same way as UNESCO (but with infinitely more style), he first turns man into a tribal being before attacking chauvinism and segregation.

But it would be unfair to accuse all those who promote multiculturalism of bowing to the power of the collective unconscious. Most of them do not. They do not accept tribalism nor the lyricism of terror. To keep man from being overshadowed entirely by his culture, they insist on the opposite, on the necessity of challenging the voice of instinct by teaching cultural relativism. If Europeans spontaneously love Europe better than the rest of the world, their country better than Europe, and their families better than their country, then we will train them to feel differently. We will teach Europeans to conquer their natural reflexes, their preferences.

In 1985 the Collège de France presented the president of the republic with a report entitled "Proposals for the Education of the Future." According to the most eminent academic institution in the country, the first of ten principles to which modern schools must subscribe reads as follows:

The unity of science and the plurality of cultures. A carefully fashioned system of education must be able to integrate the universalism inherent in scientific thought with the relativism of the social sciences, that is, with disciplines attentive to the significance of cultural differences among people and to the ways people live, think and feel.[10]

Since we tend to reject the Other, our schools, claim the sages of the Collège de France, or, to be more precise, the social sciences at school, must teach us to control our impulses. Why the social sciences? Because, based as they are on the comparative method, they demonstrate the arbitrary nature of our symbolic system. The social sciences intensify the transmission of our values by denouncing their historical authenticity. These disciplines catch authors in the trap of their own particularism, putting them back into the context from which they seem, at first glance, to escape. From the perspective of the social sciences, high culture is only the fragmentary expression of a far broader category that includes food, clothing, work, games, in sum "all the customs and skills learned by man as a member of a society."[11] And by *subsuming the cultured under the cultural*, the social sciences accomplish two things at once: they prevent us from being satisfied with ourselves and from making the world all over again in our own image. The social sciences cure us from imperialism and tribalism, from the belief that we are the lawful heirs of universalism and from the aggressive affirmation of our own specificity. Thanks to their teachings, our European identity is no longer a mission or a subject of pride; it is just one way of living and thinking, to be considered alongside everybody else's.

Goethe, then, must confront the exoticism of the Chinese novel with which he felt so naively at home. In reading this piece of literature, written in a place far away, we recall that Goethe enjoyed the intoxicating sensation of leaping across time and space, of gaining access to a world beyond the diversity of nations. What gave Goethe pleasure in this book, which he happened upon by chance, was the possibility of coming into contact with people from another civilization *without having the discovery of their difference diminish the meaning of communication*. Having no pity, the social sciences dispel this illusory sense of closeness, interrupt the conversation and return everyone back home: *Hermann and Dorothea* to the Germany of 1800, the Chinese novel to the Far East from which it came. In doing away with distinctions between works of art and documents, Goethe's dream of a universal literature disappears as well.

A curious rejection. For in charging the social sciences with the task of teaching relativism, the sages of the Collège de

France are pursuing the same objective as Goethe: to persuade people that "there is no such thing as a patriotic art or science." Although the goal is the same, the arguments used underline their differences. According to Goethe, "like every good thing, art and science belong to the entire world."[12] On the one hand beauty is like a mathematical theorem: *it does not stay in one place*, it separates itself from its place of origin and generously offers itself up to the pleasures of one and all. On the other hand science does not have a monopoly on truth: great novels differ from mere archival documents because they are not simply material for historians but forms of investigation of the world and of existence. One hundred and fifty years later *the University reduces the novel to archival material*, reserving only for theorems the privilege of breaking away from the time and place of their origin. The change appears in the very first words of the report issued by the Collège de France: it is in science and science alone that man rises above the ways of thinking he inherits from the collectivity to which he belongs. When it comes to everything else—customs, institutions, beliefs, intellectual and artistic productions—he is locked into his culture. Dissident or conformist, lyrical or mocking, he is part of the whole, an element in the system, the bard of the community: to forget the innate dominance of the group leads to outbursts of pride and violence. A local language claiming universality, a province considering itself the same as the world, a passing moment taking on eternal dimensions, a cultural *difference* assuming absolute *value*: these are the kinds of dangers the social sciences must constantly watch out for and address.

Put another way, we can no longer accept the idea that there exists a concrete universal alongside the abstract universal for which mathematics offers a model. Flaubert is not an "explorer of existence,"[13] but someone who casts light on a particular situation, region, and culture as Proust and Cervantes do as well. Creations of beauty, which Goethe saw as having the marvelous power to betray their nations and give themselves over to the whole world instead, now become little more than archetypal expressions of individual traditions, limited to particular times and places. If we want to put an end to artistic patriotism, then return works of art to the countries from which they come, give them back to the group (ethnic or social) whose specificity they represent. We must learn to stop classifying art, to eliminate hierarchies that rank some works over others. We must diffuse the criteria for determining beauty and truth throughout the world (as long as they do not bear the stamp of Scientific Research) and thus do away with the grounds for making value judgments, endorsing instead the proliferation of different kinds of "cultural sensibilities."

Like Goethe, we want to eradicate cultural chauvinism, but to do so, we ask the educators of tomorrow to follow Herder instead and convert literature into folklore. In the name of difference, I, Ernest, Hippolyte, or Jules, am no longer everywhere. I inhabit the place allotted to me in the world and do not go beyond it. Aware that my opinions have their own history and territory, I have also learned to appreciate the many other cultures of the world while contenting myself to being who I am. This gives Milan, Julio, Jamila, Boris, and Rachel the possibility to exist without me, or, when circumstances demand it, to maintain their differences while living by my side.

The sages of the Collège de France remain true to the spirit of decolonization. But unlike Régis Debray they have nothing good to say about French nationalism or European particularism. Where they do join Debray, however, is in rejecting with him the idea of the cultural continuity of humanity[14] in favor of the unique and noble image of bringing people closer together.

Culture in Pieces

The educational system of tomorrow should try "to break with the ethnocentric vision of humanity which sees Europe at the origin of all discoveries and all measures of progress."[15] This desire, it would appear, belongs to the great critical tradition introduced to Europe at the beginning of the modern period. "We are all so wrapped up and blinded by who we are, that we cannot see beyond the ends of our noses," observed Montaigne in the sixteenth century, as he assigned to education the role to correct this shortsightedness: to undo the spontaneous attachment individuals had to the places where they were born by giving them the skills to ask questions and to doubt.

But appearances are sometimes deceiving. By proclaiming the uniqueness of every culture, by excluding science and science alone from the law of relativity, the report prepared by the Collège de France repudiates the spirit of modernity and, in the name of toleration, questions the very values associated with the period.

Tolerance versus humanism: this is the way we might summarize the paradoxical critique of ethnocentrism that ends up defining individuals by their culture. To speak of culture only in the plural is to refuse people of different periods or civilizations the possibility to communicate about values and meaning beyond the limits of the place where they first appear. Far from denying that it could occur, the modern period transferred the possibility of such communication from *religion* to *culture*. As Milan Kundera rightly observes, "In the modern period, when the medieval God was transformed into *Deus absconditus*, religion relinquished its place to culture and the latter became the realization of the supreme values by which European humanity understood, defined, and identified itself."[16] Goethe himself was only claiming the privilege of universality for the most beautiful works of art, a privilege previously reserved for the divine word alone. God may have been eclipsed, but not "the gift, perhaps supernatural, to see the similarity of one man to another underneath the diversity of historical traditions that each one continues to practice."[17] As the Book of Books lost its special position and joined the ranks of one book among others, all literature, including the Bible, became the place where foreign sensibilities encountered one another, where individual spirits showed their ability to pass through history without losing themselves entirely. Critical inquiry, the enlightenment of science, the free pursuit of understanding led to the *profanation* of revealed texts; the *promotion* of literature claimed the unity of the human species and rejected particularisms. As argumentation replaced tradition, and freedom of spirit religious authority, the biblical period came to an end, at least in one sense. In another, it continued, for the word, uprooted, maintained its power.[18]

In the century when nationalism reigned, France—to its credit and originality—refused to accept the idea that the spirit had ethnic roots. The country's loyalty to universalistic principles earned the admiration not long ago of Witold Gombrowicz. He used the case of France as a corrective to Poles, who, fascinated by their "Polishness," were wearing themselves out trying to become the best examples possible of their collective history: "Is a Frenchman more French if he sees nothing but France or less French? To be really French means to see something beyond France."[19] An admirable observation and one that explains why France for many years has attracted foreigners chased from their homes by the hateful stupidity of the Volksgeist. Emmanuel Lévinas, for example, who left Lithuania in 1923, chose to study at the University of Strasbourg because "France is a country in which attachment to cultural forms appears to be the same thing as attachment to the land."[20] *France cannot be reduced to Frenchness*, its patrimony to unconscious choices or to typical and inherited ways of being. France is made up of a set of values offered to human intelligence. Lévinas himself became French out of his love for Molière, Descartes, Pascal, and Malebranche, whose works did not cultivate the picturesque, but considered something other than France and made original contributions to universal literature or philosophy.

Today this ideal is going out of fashion. Supporters of multiculturalism are finishing the task that nationalists never completed, accomplishing with expressions of humility what arrogant defenders of "God and Country" failed to achieve:

While granting the Other the freedom to be other, multiculturalists return to the uniqueness of their nation; they look, as others do, at the unique spirit of their people. Defining France (and by extension Europe) by *its* culture, they no longer recognize the central place *culture* has in society. They describe their people as having distinct characteristics, but with fierce determination demonstrate how they take no pride in the ways they are different.

Are we living out simultaneously the final chapters in the history of the biblical and modern periods? Yes or no; to reply by saying, "We are only one culture," is not an answer but a capitulation, affirming the glorious and triumphant success of identity politics. In their attempt to make the Old World welcoming at last, the apostles of multiculturalism have quite consciously destroyed the spirit of Europe, making prosperity the only attraction Europe has left.

The Right to Be a Servant

Another characteristic of the modern period in Europe is the priority given to individuals over the social groups to which they belong. Human collectivities are no longer conceived as totalities that assign to individuals identities that never change, but as associations of independent people. This great shift in perspective does not do away with social hierarchies, but it profoundly modifies the way we look at situations of inequality. A society based on individuals is still made up of rich and poor, masters and servants, but—and this change is revolutionary—there is no longer any recognition of natural differences between them: "It may be that one of them commands, but let it be clear that it might just as well have been the other way round; let it also be understood and recorded that in no way, in the name of no intrinsic or inborn sense of superiority, does one exercise authority over the other."[21]

Up until then individuals had their place in the social order defined for them. Now, all of a sudden, they can leave their assigned position. They become casteless and win, as Ernst Bloch magnificently puts it, "the right to reject their uniform."[22] Robes no longer make the monk. Man appears in his original nakedness, identified no longer by his place in the social hierarchy, cut off from his clan, guild, and lineage. While rejecting all reference to religion, the modern period fulfills the biblical revelation: all humanity is one.

As we have seen, the idea of the Volksgeist came into being with the explicit goal of putting an end to this scandal and of clothing individuals once again: Persians, Frenchmen, Spaniards, or Germans, we each have a national uniform and an obligation to our country to fulfill scrupulously the task assigned to us by history. In exchange for giving historical right the place previously held by divine right, the collectivity has taken its revenge: the casteless have been reintegrated and have put their uniforms back on.

The alternative, then, is simple: either people have rights or they have uniforms; either they can legitimately free themselves from oppression, even (and especially) if their ancestors had already been subjugated and were bearing the burden, or else their culture has the last word. As Marx warns in his vigorous critique of those who defend traditions over individuals, the serf whipped by the knout is forced to choke back his cries of rebellion and suffering, "once that knout has become time-honored, ancestral and historical."[23]

Today the opposition is confused: supporters of a multicultural society demand the right of everybody to wear a uniform. In their laudable desire to give people back their identity, they have conflated two schools of thought with conflicting perspectives: natural rights and historical rights.

Then, in a singular feat of reasoning, they present as the ultimate achievement of individual freedom the absolute dominance of the collectivity: "To help the immigrants, we must first of all respect them as they are and as they want to be according to their national identity, their cultural specificity, their spiritual and religious heritage."[24]

But what if a culture teaches people to inflict corporal punishment on delinquents, to reject barren women, to kill adulterous women, to consider the testimony of one man the same as the testimony of two women, to give a sister only half as much inheritance as her brother, to perform female circumcision, to forbid mixed marriages and permit polygamy? To love our neighbor must we respect these customs? If the answer is yes, then we seem to be saying that the serf should be able to benefit from the knout, that to deprive her of this would mutilate her being, threaten her dignity as a person, give evidence, in other words, of our racism.

In a world deserted by transcendence, fanatics no longer evoke the name of God to justify barbaric customs; they call on identity politics instead. Unable to appeal to heaven, they defend their beliefs with history and difference. God is dead, but the Volksgeist lives on, even though the idea of the rights of man came into existence precisely to challenge the authority of traditions deeply entrenched in the soil of the Old Continent. It was *at the expense of their culture* that European individuals gained, one by one, all their rights. In the end it is the critique of tradition that constitutes the spiritual foundation of Europe, a fact the philosophy of decolonization has let us forget by persuading us that the individual is nothing more than a cultural phenomenon.

"Europe," Julien Benda wrote in 1933,

will be a product of your spirit, of the will of your spirit, not a product of your being. And if you reply that you do not believe in the autonomy of the spirit, that your spirit cannot be anything other than an aspect of your being, then I say to you that you will never make Europe happen. For there is no such thing as a European *being*.[25]

Put to the test of the Other, the questioning of the being by the spirit became the distinctive sign of a particular kind of being of a precise ethnic group. The act of refusing to assimilate what is good to what is ancestral became a trait of civilization; the revolt against tradition was transformed into a European custom. Many Europeans recognize that Europe and Europe alone

ranked the individual above all else. But they apologize immediately for having done so: "there is nothing to be proud of.
Having wanted to convert the planet to our whims, we have
caused too much irreparable damage. The time of the Crusades
is over; we will no longer force anyone to adopt our view of
society." Ashamed of the way we have dominated the peoples
of the third world for so long, we swear not to begin again and,
to demonstrate our resolve, we choose to excuse others for not
meeting the standards of European-style freedom. For fear of
doing violence to individual immigrants, we confuse these new
arrivals with the uniform fashioned for them by history. To let
them live as they like, we refuse to protect them from the mis-
deeds or eventual abuses they might experience at the hands of
their own traditions. Attempting to minimize the brutal experience of leaving home, we turn immigrants over, bound hand
and foot, to other members of their community who are living
abroad. In doing so we end up limiting the application of the
rights of man only to societies identified with the West, believing all the time that we have expanded these rights by giving
peoples of other traditions the chance to live by the laws of
their own cultures.

Born out of the struggle for the emancipation of peoples,
cultural relativism has become a celebration of servitude. Must
we therefore go back to old assimilationist solutions and separate new arrivals from their religion or ethnic group? Is the end
of any sense of a collective conscience the price we must pay
for integration? *Absolutely not.* Treating foreigners as individuals
does not require forcing them to adopt all the customs prac-

ticed by the culture of the new land. We can denounce the inequality that exists between men and women in aspects of Islamic tradition without it meaning that we want to dress Muslim immigrants in a new uniform or destroy their community ties. Only those who reason according to the logic of cultural identity (and therefore of cultural integrality) believe that the national collectivity must make other communities disappear for the sake of its own survival. As far as it is concerned, the spirit of modern Europe accommodates itself very well to the existence of ethnic or religious minorities, on condition that they conform to the model of a nation comprised of free and equal individuals. This demand carries along with it the rejection of all practices—including those whose roots go deep into history—that reject the basic rights of human beings.

It is undeniable that the presence in Europe of a growing number of immigrants from the third world poses a new set of problems. Driven from their homes by poverty and traumatized by the humiliation of colonialism, these people cannot feel the same kind of attraction and gratitude for the country taking them in that most refugees from Eastern Europe experienced earlier this century. Envied for its wealth, hated for its imperialistic past, the haven now opening its doors to them is not the promised land. One thing, however, is clear: we will never resolve the difficulties facing us by allowing the need to abolish privileges to become the prerogative of one civilization alone. We cannot limit the practice of individual rights and what Toqueville calls "the equality of conditions" only to those we identify with the West.

PART FOUR

WE ARE THE WORLD,
WE ARE THE CHILDREN

A Pair of Boots Is Worth a Play by Shakespeare

Those who defend the rights of third world peoples are not alone in advocating that European nations become multicultural societies. The prophets of *postmodernity* have the same goal. But while the former defend the equality of all traditions in the face of Western arrogance, the latter challenge the search for cultural roots, in the first place, maintaining instead the dizzying fluidity of all peoples.

Postmodernist social actors draw on a notion that first appeared in the art world. Substituting eclecticism for tradition, they apply to their lives principles held by architects and painters who use the same name. They combine distinct styles, instead of insisting on a single one, and refuse to make the brutal choice between lining up with the established academy or with innovation. Rather than decide between classical or avant-garde, bourgeois or bohemian, they combine the most disparate and passing fads, the most contradictory inspirations. Free of any fixed system of beliefs, they move easily from one thing to another: from a Chinese restaurant to a West Indian night club, from couscous to cassoulet, from jogging to religion, from literature to hang gliding.

"Enjoy yourself," is the motto of this new kind of hedonism, of a way of life that rejects both nostalgia and self-criticism. The followers of postmodernism do not dream of an *authentic* society, where people live comfortably in their cultural identities, but a *polymorphous* one, a multicolored, heterogeneous world in which individuals have many lifestyles to choose from. They have less interest in promoting the right to be different than the right to have access to the differences of others. For them multicultural means *a storehouse of options*. Instead of appreciating cultures as cultures, in their entirety, they prefer to look at bits and pieces they can try on for a while, taste and enjoy, and then throw away. Consumers, not preservers of existing traditions, they vigorously object to any obstacle placed in the way of diversity by rigid and worn out ideologies.

Indulged children of affluent societies join forces with critics of the West, and together they proclaim: "All cultures are equally legitimate; everything is cultural." But their single voice obscures the fact that they have very different positions. The philosophy of decolonization has taken up the cry against art and thought first expressed by Russian populists in the nineteenth century: "A pair of boots is worth more than a play by Shakespeare." These boots are not only better than Elizabethan plays at protecting the unfortunate from the cold, they are also morally superior: they do not lie. Boots are what they are: modest products of a particular culture. They do not pretend to be official works of art, piously hiding their origins, forcing everyone to respect them. And their sense of humility should serve as a model: if art does not want to go down in history as an imposture, it should turn its back on Shakespeare and draw as close as it can to the pair of boots.

When it comes to painting, minimalists have responded to the challenge by eliminating creative gestures, exhibiting works in museums that can hardly be distinguished from the objects and materials of everyday life. To do the same writers should adopt the canons of "lesser" forms of literature that express the voice of the people and reject the hallowed texts that express only the individual, isolated in his genius, separated from others by a pseudomastery of style. Writers must free themselves from a terrible kind of asceticism, the affliction of authors in advanced, so-called cultured nations. In order to achieve the cultural simplicity of a pair of boots, those raised in privileged societies have, as a result, a longer way to go than inhabitants of developing nations. But have no fear!

Even he who has the misfortune of being born in a country with a great literary tradition is forced to use [the dominant] language, like a Czech Jew who writes in German, or a man from Uzbek in Russian; like a dog digging a hole, or a rat burrowing in. Thus it is necessary to find one's own point of underdevelopment, one's own patois, one's own third world, one's very own desert.[1]

In postmodern thought the argument is different. Raging nihilism makes it possible to admire equally the author of *King Lear* and Charles Jourdan. As long as they carry the name of a great designer, a pair of boots is worth a play by Shakespeare. And in keeping with this, a comic strip that combines an exciting love story with beautiful pictures is worth a novel by Nabokov; these little Lolitas are the same as *Lolita*; a clever piece of advertising is worth a poem by Apollinaire or Francis Ponge; the rhythm of a rock song, a melody by Duke Ellington; a beautiful soccer match, a ballet by Pina Bausch; a great couturier, Manet, Picasso, or Michelangelo; contemporary opera—"about life, a music video, a jingle, a spot"[2]—is basically the same as Verdi or Wagner. The soccer player and the choreographer, the painter and the couturier, the writer and the ideas man, the musician and the rock star are all in the same way *creative artists*. We must stop clinging to academic prejudices that reserve the title *artist* only for certain people and demote all others to a subcultural category instead.

Rather than humbling Shakespeare, we ennoble the boot maker. We are not desecrating high culture, reducing it to the level of common acts performed daily in the shadows by average men. On the contrary, we have made it possible for sports, fashion, leisure activities to force open the doors of culture. The vengeful or masochistic assimilation of the cultured (the life of the mind) into the cultural (daily customs) is replaced by a sort of joyous confusion that elevates every practice to the ranks of great human creations.

The words may be the same, but postmodern thought has broken completely with the philosophy of decolonization. Defenders of third world peoples see themselves as inconsolable widowers of an authoritarian age, the way humanists and proponents of racial and cultural purity do. Some of them (from Herder to Lévi-Strauss) want to give men back their lost uniforms; others (from Goethe to Renan) invite people to disrobe only to confine them immediately to another uniform: what is the use of challenging Tradition if it only leads to replacing custom with the indisputable authority of Culture?

Between someone like Barrès, who locks individuals into their specificity, and Benda, who prescribes for all people the same, ritualized canonical course, no matter where they come from, where is progress?

Introducing a new ideal model, postmodern antiracism pushes Benda, Barrès, and Lévi-Strauss out of fashion, replacing all three of them with *the multicultural individual.*

The notion of identity has grown extremely complicated. Our roots go back to Montaigne studied at school, to Mourousi and television, to Touré Kunda, to reggae music, Renaud and Lavilliers.[3] We do not need to see if we have lost our cultural references, because we have many different points of reference. We have the luck to live in a country at the crossroads, where freedom of speech and thought is respected. Cultural references for us are a mixture, a crossbreeding of traditions.[4]

Consider yourself warned: if you believe that confused thinking protects no one from xenophobia; if you insist on maintaining a firm set of values; if you react negatively to the triumph of those who make no distinctions; if you refuse to put the author of *Essays* in the same cultural category as a television personality, to see a meditation created to awaken the spirit in the same light as a show made to dull it; if you refuse to equate Beethoven and Bob Marley, even though one of them is white and the other black, then you line up hopelessly on the side of the pricks and wet blankets. You are a moral crusader and your attitude is criminal three times over: 1) As a puritan, you stand in the way of all life's pleasures. 2) As a despot, you thunder forth against those who refuse your prix fixe menu in favor of one with selections à la carte—you have only one wish: to stop the march toward human autonomy. 3) Finally, you share with racists a phobia for mixing and a belief in discriminatory policies. Instead of openly supporting the latter, you oppose the former.[5]

What does postmodern thought want? The same thing as the Enlightenment: to make man independent, to treat him like an adult, in sum, to speak like Kant, to move him out of his condition of childhood for which he himself is responsible. From the perspective of postmodernism, people will make a decisive step toward becoming adults the day they stop ranking intellectual activities as superior to other ways of spending time, when they begin considering the life of the mind no different from betting at the race track or listening to rock and roll. To enter the new age of autonomy, we must turn all *obligations* dating from the period of authoritarianism into some of the many *options* now open to us.

Elitism remains the enemy, but the meaning of the word has surreptitiously been reversed. By saying: "We must do for culture what Jules Ferry did for public education," André Malraux placed himself explicitly in the Enlightenment tradition and tried to generalize the knowledge of the great works of mankind; today the books of Flaubert find themselves relegated to the peaceful world of leisure, together with pulp novels, TV shows, and schmaltzy films intoxicated with contemporary incarnations of Emma Bovary. To be elitist (therefore intolerable) is no longer a matter of refusing to give culture to the people but of refusing to apply the label "cultural" to any form of distraction that may come along. We are living in a time of *feelings*, where there is no truth or lie, no stereotype or invention, nothing beautiful or ugly, but an infinite palette of different and equal pleasures. Democracy used to mean culture was accessible to everybody; now it implies that everyone has a right to the culture of his or her choice (or to identify as cultural any urge of the moment).

"Let me do what I want to do."[6] No transcendent authority, neither historical nor representative, can inflict its preferences on postmodern subjects or govern their actions. Provided with remote control buttons for life and TV, they turn on their program with a calm soul, no longer intimidated by traditional hierarchies. Free in the sense Nietzsche means when he says that you have achieved freedom when you are no longer embarrassed by yourself, postmodern subjects can *let everything go* and give in to immediate delights. Rimbaud or Renaud, Lévinas or Lavilliers, whatever they decide, the choice they make is cultural.

The absence of thought [*la non-pensée*] has of course always coexisted with the life of the mind, but this is the first time in European history that the two share same the name (*culture*) and enjoy the same status. Those who believe in "high" culture and dare make the distinction are called racists or reactionaries.

Let us be clear: dissolving culture into the cultural has not put an end to intellectual or artistic work. No need to lament nostalgically about a golden age when people produced masterpieces by the thousands. As old as resentment, this cliché goes back to the beginnings of the spiritual life of mankind. But the problem facing us this time is different and more serious: the works exist, but the boundary between culture and entertainment has been blurred. There is no longer any place to receive these pieces of art and give them meaning. Thus they float absurdly in space without coordinates or points of reference. Once hating culture becomes cultural in itself, the life of the mind loses all significance.

When Ulrich heard about a *brilliant* racing horse for the first time, he, not having the qualities of Musil, gave up his ambitions forever. This was in 1913, and Ulrich was a promising young scientist with aspirations of joining the world of intellectuals. But why bother anymore?

In his imprisoned youth, Ulrich had hardly ever heard people speak about anything but women and horses. He had fled all that in order to become a great man. And then, after having accomplished many different things, at the very moment he could feel himself reaching his goal, the horse got there first and saluted him from below.[7]

Less radical than his hero, Musil wrote the first two volumes of *The Man Without Qualities.* He has, so it seems, been rewarded for perseverance. Nobody questions his genius anymore. Dead and forgotten for many years, he now appears in exhibitions, his works come out in new editions, academics study him, all as part of the fascination people have today for the last years of the Austro-Hungarian Empire. But—and this is the irony of history—the pessimism evoked by the character of Ulrich is confirmed by the way his creator is commemorated. As Guy Scarpetta noted, the style of Vienna, seen from this end of the twentieth century, is characterized by "a sort of leveling, the flattening out of proper names one on top of the other—offering one more way of presenting 'Vienna' as a homogeneous block."[8] From ornamental kitsch to the emperor's sideburns, anything to do with Frantz-Josef becomes the object of veneration. A famous indiscriminate cult, *The Man Without Qualities* and Strauss's waltzes. We love in Vienna the anticipated image of our own confusion. After having triumphed, the new spirit, denounced by Musil, pays the author solemn homage.

There are no accursed poets any more. Allergic to all forms of exclusion, the dominant view of culture does away with making distinctions between Shakespeare and Musil on the one hand, and boots and racing horses on the other. They are all equally valued.

His Majesty the Consumer

Do not think, however, that qualities painfully lacking today were abundant in the past. No nineteenth-century bourgeois would ever have called a racing horse "brilliant" or extolled the beauty of a pair of boots. But in refusing to do so, he would have spoken in the name of utilitarianism, not humanism. His profound distrust of any leisure activity had nothing to do with an enlightened view of culture. "Do not forget that time is money"! Adopting this law as his holy commandment and a business mentality as his only form of reason, the bourgeois made no distinctions: he condemned as equally frivolous and wasteful artistic endeavors, spectator sports, and fancy clothing. Seeing the world in purely *technological* terms, he only had patience for practical activities and useful knowledge. Everything else was literature. In sum, it was instrumental reason or "calculative thinking," to use Heidegger's phrase, that relegated meditative thinking (what we are calling culture) to the realm of entertainment: "Technology as the highest form of rational consciousness, technologically interpreted, and the lack of reflection as the arranged powerlessness, opaque to itself, to attain a relation to what is worthy of question, belong together: they are the same thing."[9]

Major upheavals have occurred since then; once needs and desires were rigorously controlled; now they receive solicitous attention. Vice becomes virtue. Advertising replaces asceticism, and the spirit of capitalism inspires the relentless pursuit of life's immediate delights from the moment of birth. Extraordinary as it may seem, this ideological revolution maintains deep ties to the Puritan tradition. By saying simultaneously: "Get rich!" and "Have fun!" by making free time profitable in lieu of condemning it, present-day hedonism turns bourgeois reason against the bourgeois: calculative thinking overcomes its previous tendency to be exclusive; it discovers the usefulness of the useless; it methodically invests in appetites and pleasures and, after having reduced culture to an unproductive waste of time, it awards all forms of distraction with the status of culture. No transcendent value should stand in the way or determine how people use leisure and develop a taste for consumption.

But—and this difference makes the world of yesterday superior, relatively speaking, to the world of today—men of culture used to fight against the tyranny of calculative thinking and call it stupid. In contrast, their postmodern descendants make practically no objections. What is more, while yesterday's Artist declared war on the Philistine he still worried about becoming elitist and abandoning the elementary principles of democracy. Today's intellectual bows to the powerful will of show business, fashion, and advertisement and says not a word. Even ministers of culture remain silent, for they have rapidly transformed themselves into managers of leisure.

In writing about the American cinema in the early 1960s, Hannah Arendt was already saying, "There are many great authors of the past who have survived centuries of oblivion and neglect, but it is still an open question whether they will be able to survive an entertaining version of what they have to say."[10] Less than thirty years later Hollywood producers are not the only ones watering down works like *Doctor Zhivago*—avant-garde theater directors are doing the same by bringing music hall and television aesthetics to the stage. And still almost nobody objects.

Intellectuals do not worry anymore about the survival of culture. Is this their latest betrayal? Whatever it may be, the culture industry encounters no resistance when it invests in culture and claims for itself all the prestige of creation.

Nobody, it is true, can fight on all fronts at once, and today's intellectuals have chosen to go to war against "the moralizing masochism"[11] of preceding generations: abandoning Marx by means of Tocqueville, they show that democracy does not obscure exploitation and the class struggle, but constitutes, on the contrary, the great anthropological mutation of modern societies. Different from all other categories of human beings, democratic man conceives of himself as an independent person—as a social atom. Separated from his ancestors, his contemporaries, and his descendants, all at the same time, his primary concern is to provide for his private needs and to see himself equal to all other people. Instead of slandering him, we must defend this precarious creature against his enemies, these neo-Tocquevillians add, and against that part of himself which dreams of returning

to the good old times when everybody thought the same way, when everyone's place was clear, and sense of belonging tangible, when complementary interests converged, without competing, when one and all moved smoothly toward a single and manifest goal and formed the solid frame of a communitarian existence.[12]

Totalitarian regimes give evidence of what happens to democratic man when he succumbs to this kind of nostalgia.

Such a rehabilitation of Western individualism would deserve enthusiastic applause, if it did not, in a moment of self-congratulatory rage, confuse egoism (or, to use a circumlocution stripped of all moral connotations, the state of everyone for himself) with autonomy.

But the fact that an individual has broken the ties that used to attach him to old communitarian structures (corporations,

122

churches, castes, or hierarchical rankings) and has managed his affairs with no restrictions, does not ipso facto give him new direction in the world. He can cut himself off from society without being free of its prejudices. Limiting authority does not guarantee independence of judgment or will. When inherited social constraints disappear, there is no assurance that freedom of the spirit will follow. It is still necessary to have what people called enlightenment in the eighteenth century: "As long as there are people who do not think for themselves, who let others make up their minds for them, breaking the chains is all in vain."[13]

In a single breath Enlightenment philosophers fought to give everyone access to culture while releasing the individual from the power of the state and the control of tradition. They wanted men to be free to do what was good for themselves but also to think about matters beyond the limits of their own self-interest.

We see today that the philosophers won only half the battle. Despotism has been vanquished, but not obscurantism. While traditions have lost their power, so has culture. People, it is true, are not deprived of knowledge. Quite the reverse. In fact we might say that in the West and for the first time in history, the spiritual and intellectual heritage of mankind is available, immediately and in its entirety. Now that paperbacks, videocassettes, and data banks have taken over the cottage industry created by the *Encyclopédistes*, there are no longer any material obstacles standing in the way of spreading the Enlightenment. However, just as technology—television and computers—is able to introduce all forms of knowledge into every home, the

123

logic of consumption destroys culture. The word lives on, but emptied of any idea of education, of the possibility of opening up to the world and caring for the soul. From now on in, the pleasure principle—self-interest in its postmodern form—dominates the individual's spiritual life. It is no longer a question of representing men as autonomous subjects, but of gratifying their immediate desires and providing them with entertainment for very little cost. With this careless conglomeration of random and passing needs, the postmodern individual has forgotten that freedom means more than having the power to switch channels on the TV, and culture more than satisfying an urge.

Even the clearest, most disenchanted critics of the times have forgotten. When they speak about the "era of emptiness," they still describe it as an important step forward, the final stage, some say, of democracy. They may talk ironically of the "kaleidoscopic age of supermarkets and self-service restaurants,"[14] but they offer the world no alternative to this relationship other than the threat of orderly discipline and the rigor of conventions. Sweet regression, they believe, is better than bitter repression. It even offers protection: "No need to despair, 'the weakening of the will' is not catastrophic, it does not create a subjected and alienated people, nor does it announce the rise of totalitarianism: relaxed apathy represents even more of a defense against eruptions of historical religiosity and grand paranoiac plans."[15]

Previously blind *to* totalitarianism, now reason is blinded by it. The crimes of the imperialistic West obscured for a long time the monstrosities committed in the name of revolution. From now on Big Brother serves as an alibi and foil for the disappearance of culture in the West. The specter of 1984 turns us into *Panglosses of the consumer society*: the violent intrusions of power into our private lives justify the smiling aggression of Muzak and advertising. Caught by everything and nothing in the Disneyland of culture, forced indoctrination of the masses makes the dilemmas of individuals seem like supreme exercises in autonomy; it makes a world guided by remote control the best of all possible arrangements.[16]

"A Society That Has Finally Become Adolescent"

The ignorant cannot be free. Or so the philosophers of the Enlightenment believed. You are not born an individual, they used to say, you become one by rising above the disorderliness of appetites, the narrowness of self-interest, and the tyranny of received ideas. The logic of consumerism leads to a different conclusion: freedom and culture define ways of satisfying needs, not of controlling them. That man might have to resist his natural desires and break with tradition in order to become an autonomous subject *is an idea that has vanished from the very vocabulary used to describe the independent subject*. Hence the crisis in education. School, in the modern sense of the term, was born in the Age of Enlightenment. Today it is dying, as people question the values of that period. There now exists a huge gap between a common code of ethics and that place governed by the strange idea that there is no autonomy without thinking and no thinking without self-discipline. The mental life of society develops "in a middle zone of personal eclecticism,"[17] everywhere, that is, except between the four walls of educational institutions. School is the ultimate exception to the generalized rule of self-service. Thus the misunderstanding is growing, separating the institution from those who use it: the school system is modern, the students postmodern. The school wants to educate minds, but the students bring to it the attention span of young people raised on television. As the school tries, to use the words of Condorcet, to "eliminate the distinction between coarse and enlightened members of our species," students reinterpret this liberating vision as an old form of subjugation. With one sweep of the hand they reject authority, discipline, and the transmission of ideas, confusing the master who teaches with the master who dominates.

How can we resolve this contradiction? "By making schools postmodern," respond school administrators and reformers alike. The latter look for ways to bring education and consumption closer together, and have gone so far, in certain American schools, as to package grammar, history, mathematics, and other basic subjects into rock music cassettes that students listen to on their Walkmans.[18] Administrators, on the other hand, recommend more cautiously the large-scale use of computers in the classroom, hoping, in this way, to introduce high school students to the importance of technology without forcing them to leave the world of child's play. From electric trains to computers, from entertainment to intellectual activities, moving from one to the other should occur gently and, if possible, without letting those benefiting from it realize that anything has happened. What difference does it make that intelligence gained by play and machines was acquired through manipulation, not thinking? Between the ever growing role of technology in determining fields of knowledge and the multiplying varieties of consumption, the kind of judgment needed to think about the world is no longer of any use. As we have already seen, there is not even a word to describe this kind of judgment anymore, since "culture" has been confiscated for good.

But to reconcile fully school with "life," it is not enough to play around with curriculum and teaching methods. During a long and detailed study of what ails the French schools, two sociologists wrote,

If by culture we mean all those forms of behavior, technology, customs, and values that create the identity of a group, then music makes up an important part of the culture of the young. Unfortunately, their music—rock, pop, incidental—is considered by adult society and the teaching establishment in particular, as inferior music. The school curriculum, the kind of preparation music teachers receive, maintains a hierarchy that places classical works at the top. We will not even debate this point, despite the obvious false notes. What interests us here is the enormous gap that exists between the tastes of the students and the education they get.[19]

So let us just play. At school this means eliminating the gap by giving in to adolescent tastes. *Teach youthfulness to the young* instead of holding on with senile determination to outdated hierarchies. Replace Mozart on the syllabus with works by that fiery rock star Amadeus, known as Wolfie to his wife, whom he met one lovely Indian summer afternoon on a campus in Vienna, Massachusetts.

The Young are a recent development. Before there was school they did not exist. The traditional system of apprenticeship did not need to separate for several years those who were learning a trade from the rest of the world. There was no place for this long period called adolescence to unfold. With compulsory education adolescence stopped being a bourgeois privilege and became a universal condition and a way of life. Sheltered from the influence of their parents by the educational institution and from their professors by "the peer group," the young were able to build a world of their own, turning the values of the surrounding society upside down. Cool jeans instead of grown-up clothing, comic books instead of literature, rock music instead of verbal expression, the "youth culture"—this antischool culture—has been gaining ground and autonomy since the 1960s, that is, since the massive democratization of the educational system: "Like any closely knit group (American blacks, for example)," Paul Yonnet tells us,

the youth movement is a partially hidden continent, partially forbidden and incomprehensible as well to any outsider. People begrudge its special system of communication, which is very independent, largely underground, transported by rock culture where *feelings* are more powerful than words, sensation more powerful than the abstractions of language, atmosphere more powerful than real meanings and rational discourse. All these values are alien to the traditions of Western communication. They draw a thick curtain, offer an impenetrable defense to the half-hearted attempts of adults to connect. Whether you listen or play, you have got to feel "cool" or positively high. *Guitars express themselves better than words, which are old (they have a history) and cannot be trusted.*[20]

Here, at least, one thing is clear. Since culture, in its classical form, came into being with words, or language, it is problematic for two reasons: it *ages* people by providing them with a memory longer than their own lives and it *isolates* them, by condemning them to say "I," to exist, in other words, as distinct individuals. By destroying language, rock music wards off this double malediction: guitars abolish memory; this warm merging feeling replaces conversation, the means used by separate beings to relate to one another; the individual "I" dissolves ecstatically into the collectivity of Youth.

This step backward would be harmless enough if Youth were not everywhere now. In only two decades discordant beliefs have become the norm, autonomy has become hegemony, and adolescent culture the lifestyle of everyone in society. The young define fashion; the cinema and advertising prefer to speak to audiences between fifteen and twenty years old; thousands of radio stations, independently financed, almost all sing the same tune on the guitar, delighted that the age of conversation is over. It is open season for chasing away any trace of growing old. Yet less than a century ago, in this secure world described so well by Stefan Zweig, "he who wanted to grow up needed to use as many disguises as possible, to seem older than he was.... Newspapers advertised products which made a man's beard grow faster," and young doctors, fresh out of medical school, tried to gain a little weight and "wore mighty beards and gold spectacles even if their eyes did not need them, so that they could make an impression of 'experience.' "[21] Today, to be young is a categorical imperative for every generation. One neurosis replaces another. People in their forties remain teenagers. As for the Elders, they are not honored because they are knowledgeable (as in traditional societies), responsible (as in bourgeois societies), or frail (as in civilized societies). In fact they are not honored at all unless they stay young in body and spirit. In other words, this is no longer a matter of a group of adolescents hiding behind their collective identity in an attempt to escape the world, but of the world itself running frantically after adolescence. And this shift, as Fellini observed with some surprise, constitutes that great cultural revolution of the postmodern era:

I wonder what could have possibly happened at a particular moment, what kind of evil spell could have fallen upon our generation, to explain how we started, all of a sudden, to look at the young as the messengers of who knows what absolute truth. The young, the young, the young ... you would have thought that they had just arrived from outer space.... Only some form of collective madness could have made us consider children of fifteen years old as the master guardians of all truths.[22]

Indeed, what did happen? As curious as it may seem, this madness Fellini speaks of did not rise out of nothing. The ground was prepared and we could say that the long process leading Western societies to convert to the hedonism of consumption has culminated today in the idolatry of juvenile values. The Bourgeois is dead, long live the Adolescent! The bourgeois sacrificed the pleasures of life in order to accumulate wealth and put, to use Stefan Zweig's formulation, "Moral appearances above the human being," revealing in the process his impatience with both the rigidities of the moral order and the demands of thought. The adolescent, on the other hand, wants above all to have fun, to relax, to escape through leisure activities the rigors of school, and that is why the culture industry finds in the adolescent the kind of human being most closely in tune with its own essence.

This does not mean that adolescence has become the most beautiful age of life. Previously dismissed as people, today the young are dismissed as individuals. Youth, from now on, is a block, a monolith, almost a species unto itself. You can no longer be twenty years old without immediately becoming the spokesperson for an entire generation. "We, the young . . . " Your friends listen, your parents are touched, opinion research centers and the market work *together* to perpetuate this conformity, so that nobody can ever exclaim: "I am twenty. This is my age, not my being, and I will not let anyone lock me into such a deterministic view of myself."

And young people are even less likely to step out of their age group (their "bio-class," Edgar Morin would say) since adults are coming down to their level, offering them a cure for the absence of an intellectual life. We have already observed this in Education, but it also occurs in Politics, where we see political parties competing with one another for power, "modernizing" their images and messages while accusing each other of being "old fashioned." In journalism too we have recently read about the sponsor of a television and entertainment guide admitting that the magazine owed its success to the "under fifteen year olds surrounded by their mothers" and to the fact that the children were attracted to "our song, advertising, and music columns."[23] In Art and Literature we have seen a number of masterpieces in France become available in the "brief and artistic" form of the video. Morality gets packaged into huge concerts held for humanitarian causes broadcast over satellite television, and religion comes to us in world tours organized for John Paul II.

To justify promoting foolishness over thought and the infantilizing of culture, people often insist that the method works. In a period when people act first in their own self-interest—"Everyone for himself"—and choose to live in privacy, behind closed doors—linking charity to rock 'n' roll can bring in fabulous sums of money. As for the pope, while the best experts proclaim that God is dead, John Paul II attracts enormous crowds. However, looking more closely, such pragmatism turns out to be totally illusory. For example: the big concerts organized to relieve conditions in Ethiopia ended up paying for the deportation of the very populations they raised money to feed. The Ethiopian government, we suspect, diverted the funds. Nevertheless, the waste could have been avoided if the organizers and participants in the worldwide Mass had taken their eyes off the stage for a while and turned their attention, ever so slightly, to the dictatorship separating the children who were singing and dancing from those who were starving to death. The success John Paul II enjoys, on the other hand, comes from his style, not from the substance of what he says: he would arouse the same enthusiastic response if he gave women the right to have abortions and decided that priests could abandon vows of celibacy. His show, like that of other superstars, first empties the heads of his spectators of any ideas in order to *dazzle them with his performance*. He offers no message, but devours them in a great profusion of *son et lumière*. Although he may think he has only given in to fashion by adopting its form, the pope forgets, or makes believe he has forgotten, that this particular form has as its goal to wipe meaning out. When it comes to rock culture, rock charity, and rock religion, the young do not feel the impact of great speeches, rather the speeches themselves are replaced by rhythm and dance.

Standing up and challenging the rest of the world, the young did more than merely defend their tastes and values. In the admiring words of Paul Yonnet, they started to use "brain waves other than those which make language possible. There may be a generational conflict," he continues, "but there is also a conflict between the distinct hemispheres of the brain (non-verbal recognition versus speech), hemispheres that ignored each other for a long time."[24] It was a tough battle, but what passes today for communication attests to the fact that the non-verbal hemisphere won out: music videos over conversation. Society has "finally become adolescent."[25] The huge concerts may not have succeeded in getting relief to the victims of famine in Ethiopia, but they did establish an international hymn: "We are the world, we are the children."

And so as we come to the end, barbarism replaces culture. In the shadow of the great word, intolerance and infantile behavior increase. When it is not cultural identity restricting the choices an individual can make, using threats of high treason to silence expressions of doubt, irony, and reason—opinions that might separate him from the collectivity—it is the entertainment industry, the creation of the technological age, that reduces great works of art to drivel. The life of the mind has quietly moved out of the way, making room for the terrible and pathetic encounter of the fanatic and the zombie.

NOTES

Part One. The Idea of the Spirit Takes Root

1. Julien Benda, *The Treason of the Intellectuals*, trans. R. Aldington (New York: Norton, 1969), p. 59; *La Trahison des clercs* (Paris: Pauvert, 1965), p. 52.

2. Ibid., p. 18; p. 22.

3. J. Herder, "Yet Another Philosophy of History Concerning the Development of Mankind," in F. M. Barnard, trans. and ed., *J. G. Herder on Social and Political Culture* (London: Cambridge University Press, 1969).

4. Herder, quoted in Isaiah Berlin, *Vico and Herder* (London: Hogarth Press, 1976), p. 182.

5. Chamfort, quoted in Paul Bénichou, *Le Sacré de l'écrivain* (Paris: Corti, 1973), p. 30.

6. J. Sieyès, *What Is the Third Estate?* trans. M. Blondel, ed. S. E. Finer (New York: Praeger, 1964), p. 58; *Qu'est-ce que le Tiers-Etat?* (Paris: P.U.F., 1982), p. 31.

7. Denis Diderot, "Political Authority," in Lester G. Crocker, ed.,

Diderot's Selected Writings, trans. Derek Coltman (New York: Macmillan, 1966), p. 46; "Autorité politique," *L'Encyclopédie* (Paris: Editions sociales, 1984), p. 108.

8. Joseph de Maistre, *Essay on the Generative Principle of Political Constitutions*, with an introduction by C. M. Lombard (Delmar, N.Y.: Scholars Facsimilies and Reprints, 1977), p. xvii; *Oeuvres complètes* (Lyons: Vitte, 1884), 1:230.

9. De Maistre, "Divine Influence in Constitutions," *Consideration on France*, trans R. A. Lebrun (Montreal and London: McGill-Queen's University Press, 1974), p. 97; *Oeuvres complètes* (Lyons: Vitte, 1884), 1:75.

10. For Spengler, it is true, nations are not the fundamental cultural units; civilizations are. His perspective takes in much larger historical groupings than those of Joseph de Maistre. Scorning the shortsightedness of nationalist ideology, he posits the succession or confrontation of eight great cultures since the beginning of human history: Egyptian, Babylonian, Chinese, Indian, Ancient Greek, Arabic, Western, and the culture of the Maya in Central America. But this change of scale does not imply a different theoretical framework. Like the nations of de Maistre or Herder, Spengler describes his civilizations as discrete organisms, living entities "each stamping its material, its mankind, in *its own* image; each having *its own* idea, *its own* passions, *its own* death." Oswald Spengler, *The Decline of the West*, trans C. F. Atkinson (New York: Knopf, 1926), p. 21. There is a clear link, therefore, between the philosophy of the counterrevolution and the anthropological relativism of Spengler.

11. De Maistre, "Divine Influence in Constitutions," p. 97.

12. De Maistre, "Des souverainetés particulières et de nations," *Oeuvres complètes* (Lyons: Vitte, 1884), 1:325.

13. De Maistre, "Préface," *Oeuvres complètes* (Lyons: Vitte, 1884), 7:39, quoted in Massimo Boffa, "Joseph de Maistre: la défense de la souveraineté," *Le Débat* (March–May 1986), no. 39, p. 90.

14. Diderot, *The Encyclopedia,* in Lester G. Crocker, ed., *Diderot's Selected Writings,* trans. Derek Coltman (New York: Macmillan, 1966), p. 86; "Eclectisme," *L'Encyclopédie* (Paris: Editions sociales, 1984), p. 148.

15. Friedrich Nietzsche, *Human, All Too Human,* trans. M. Faber and S. Lehmann (Lincoln: University of Nebraska Press, 1984), p. 14; *Humain trop humain* (Paris: Denoël, 1983), p. 19.

16. Herder, "Yet Another Philosophy of History," pp. 186–87.

17. De Maistre, "The Study of Sovereignty," in Jack Lively, ed. and trans., *The Works of Joseph de Maistre* (New York: Macmillan, 1965), p. 108; "Des origines de la souveraineté," *Oeuvres complètes* (Lyons: Vitte, 1884), 1:376.

18. Voltaire, quoted in René Pomeau, *L'Europe des lumières* (Geneva: Slatkine, 1981), p. 176.

19. "The influence of the French conservatives on social thought was substantial. We need only glance at some of the sociologists to be clear on this. Thus Saint-Simon and Comte were lavish in praise of what the latter called 'the retrograde school.' This 'immortal group under the leadership of de Maistre,' wrote Comte, 'will long deserve the gratitude of positivists.' Saint-Simon attributed to Bonald the inspiration of his interest in 'critical' or 'organic' periods of history and also in the beginnings of his proposals for 'stabilizing' industrialism and democracy." Robert A. Nisbet, *The Sociological Tradition* (New York: Basic Books, 1966), pp. 12–13.

20. H. Taine, *The Ancient Regime,* trans. J. Durand (New York: Holt, 1876), p. 233; *Les Origines de la France contemporaine,* in Jacques Julliard, *La Faute à Rousseau* (Paris: Seuil, 1985), p. 144.

AF gives the age as twenty years old, whereas our translation says twenty-one. I left it as twenty-one—Trans.

21. De Maistre, "The Study of Sovereignty," p. 95; "Des origines de la souveraineté," 1:316.

22. Jean-Pierre Rioux, "Introduction à Rémy de Gourmont," *Le Joujou patriotisme* (Paris: Pauvert, 1967).

23. Ernest Renan, "Nouvelle lettre à M. Strauss," in *Histoire et parole* (Paris: Laffont, coll. Bouquins, 1984), p. 651.

24. Fustel de Coulanges, quoted in Raoul Giradet, *Le Nationalisme français* (Paris: Seuil, coll. Points, 1983), p. 64.

25. Renan, "La Réforme intellectuelle et morale de la France," in *Histoire et parole* (Paris: Laffont, coll. Bouquins, 1984), p. 597.

26. Ibid.

27. Quoted in Raoul Giradet, *Le Nationalisme français*, p. 37. The strong sentiments expressed in this declaration should not make us forget that the return to their mother country was anything but idyllic. After these early demonstrations of patriotic enthusiasm, the assimilationist and secular policies practiced in France clashed repeatedly in the interwar period with a powerful movement for independence. But that is another story, and one that diminishes the importance of the "Declaration of Bordeaux." It is not the love of France that makes this a crucial document, but the "solemn declaration of the fact that consent is the sole ground of nationality." Jean-Marie Mayeur, "Une mémoire-frontière: l'Alsace" in Pierre Nora, ed., *Les Lieux de mémoire, La Nation* (Paris: Gallimard, 1986), 2:88.

28. Renan, "What Is a Nation?" in *The Poetry of the Celtic Races and Other Studies*, trans. W. E. Hutchinson (London: Walter Scott, 1896), p. 81; "Qu'est-ce qu'une nation?" in *Oeuvres complètes* (Paris: Calmann-Lévy, 1947), 1:904.

29. Renan, "The Part of the Semitic People in the History of Civilization," *Essays in Religious History and Criticism*, trans. O. B. Frothingham (New York: Carlton, 1864), p. 165; "Discours d'ouverture au Collège de France," *Oeuvres complètes*, 8:333.

30. Renan, "Histoires des langues sémitiques," *Oeuvres complètes*, 8:146.

31. Léon Poliakov, *The Aryan Myth: A History of Racist and Nationalist Ideas in Europe*, trans. E. Howard (New York: Basic Books, 1974), p. 206; *Le Mythe aryen* (Paris: Calmann-Lévy, 1971), p. 208.

32. Renan, "What Is a Nation?" p. 77; 1:900.

33. Ibid., p. 77; 1:901.

34. Johann Peter Eckermann, in J. K. Moorhead, ed., *Conversations with Goethe*, trans. J. Oxenford (New York: Dutton, [1930] 1970), p. 165; *Conversations de Goethe avec Eckermann* (Paris: Gallimard, 1941), p. 158.

35. Goethe, *Goethe's Autobiography: Poetry and Truth From My Own Life*, trans. R. O. Moon (Washington, D.C.: Public Affairs Press, 1949), p. 337; *Poésie et vérité* (N.p.: Signe, 1960), 2:159.

36. Goethe, "On German Architecture," in John Cage, ed. and trans., *Goethe on Art* (Berkeley: University of California Press, 1980), p. 109; "Architecture allemande," in *Ecrits sur l'art* (Paris: Klincksieck, 1983), p. 72. Note that, despite the similarity of their titles, these two collections are different.

37. Goethe, "On German Architecture," p. 109; "Architecture allemande," p. 72.

38. Antoine Berman, *The Experience of the Foreign: Culture and Translation in Romantic Germany*, trans. S. Heyveaert (Albany: State University of New York Press, 1992); *L'Épreuve de l'étranger* (Paris: Gallimard, 1984).

39. Goethe, *Ecrits sur l'art,* p. 52.

40. Ibid.

41. Renan, "What Is a Nation?" p. 70; 1:895.

42. Ibid., p. 74; 1:898.

43. Renan, "Nouvelle lettre à M. Strauss," *Oeuvres complètes*, 1:651.

44. J. -L. Talmon, "Herder et la mentalité allemande," *Destin d'Israël* (Paris: Calmann-Lévy), p. 224.

45. Renan, "Lettre à M. Strauss," p. 652.

46. Vacher de la Pouge, quoted in Zeev Sternhell, *La Droite révolutionnaire, 1885–1914 (Les Origines françaises du fascisme)* (Paris: Seuil, 1978), p. 168.

47. Ibid., p. 150.

48. Joseph Gonliev Agathon, *Les Jeunes gens d'aujourd'hui,* réponse d'Henri Hoppenot, quoted in Giradet, *Le Nationalisme français*, p. 228.

49. Renan, "What Is a Nation?" p. 83.

50. Barrès, quoted in Zeev Sternhell, *La Droite révolutionnaire*, p. 162. My critics will object and say that Barrès considered Renan to be one of his masters and that he went so far as to borrow—almost word for word—his definition of national sentiment: "A nation," he declared, right in the middle of the Dreyfus affair, "is the possession of an ancient cemetery and the will to continue to value this indivisible inheritance." We should not, however, be taken in by the similarities here. While the will, for Renan, separated men from their cultural unconscious, for Barrès it tied them to it definitively: "Everything we are is born of the historical and geographic conditions of our country. Throughout the centuries, our parents have meditated over us. So that we may develop and find happiness, it is necessary that things remain essentially the same as they were when our forebears 'meditated' over us. *I need someone to watch over the tree of my culture which allowed me, weak little leaf that I am, to go so high.*" Very conscious of the philosophical differences between them, despite similarities in language and vocabulary, Barrès criticized Renan explicitly for believing "that an independent reason exists in each one of us, permitting us access to truth." He went so far as to blame his distinguished predecessor for the rise of the Dreyfus movement: "Need we say it, a man from Lorraine, who wrote *Les Déracinés*, imposes this definition on France: 'What is a nation? It is a spirit.' Now there is a formula from which we can draw, *from which we are drawing today detestable consequences.*" *Scènes et doctrines du nationalisme* (Paris: Plon, 1925), 1:114, 132, 17, 84. AF's italics.

51. Benda, *La Jeunesse d'un clerc* (Paris: Gallimard, 1964), p. 114.

52. Benda, *The Treason of the Intellectuals*, p. 95; pp. 80–81.

53. Ibid., p. 183; p. 152.

Part Two. Generous Betrayal

1. Torres Bodet, Conference for the Establishment of the United Nations Educational, Scientific, and Cultural Organization (London: Preparatory Commission of UNESCO, 1946), p. 36; Conférence des

Nations unies en vue de la création d'une organisation des Nations unies pour la science et la culture (London, 1945), p. 50.

2. Léon Blum, Conference for the Establishment of the United Nations Educational, Scientific, and Cultural Organization (London: Preparatory Commission of UNESCO, 1946), p. 22; Conférence des Nations unies en vue de la création d'une organisation des Nations unies pour la science et la culture (London, 1945), p. 34. AF attributes the quote to Clement Attlee. The English translation of the text attributes it to Blum.

3. Condorcet, *Sur la nécessité de l'instruction publique*, quoted in Catherine Kintzler, *Condorcet: L'Instruction publique et la naissance du citoyen* (Paris: Le Sycomore, 1984), p. 270.

4. Lévi-Strauss, "Race and History," *Structural Anthropology*, trans. Monique Layton, 2 vols. (Chicago: University of Chicago Press, 1976), 2:324; "Race et histoire," 2 vols. *Anthropologie structurale* (Paris: Plon, 1973), 2:378.

5. Ibid., p. 330; 2:385.

6. Lewis Henry Morgan, "Preface," *Ancient Society* (New York: Macmillan, 1877), pp. iv–v.

7. Lévi-Strauss, *The View from Afar*, trans. J. Neugroschel and P. Hoss (New York: Basic Books, 1985), p. 26; *Le Regard éloigné* (Paris: Plon, 1983), p. 50.

8. Lévi-Strauss, *Tristes Tropiques*, trans. J. and D. Weightman (New York: Washington Square Press, 1977); *Tristes Tropiques* (Paris: Plon, 1955).

9. Lévi-Strauss, "Race and History," p. 330; p. 384.

10. Michel Foucault, "Nietzsche, Geneology, History," in Paul Rabinow, ed., *The Foucault Reader*, trans. D. F. Bouchard and S. Simon (New York: Pantheon, 1984), p. 88; "Nietzsche, la généalogie, l'histoire," *Hommage à Jean Hyppolite* (Paris: P.U.F., 1971), p. 160.

11. Pierre Bourdieu and Jean-Claude Passeron, *Reproduction in Education, Society, and Culture*, trans. by Richard Nice (London and Beverly Hills: Sage, 1977), p. 8; *Eléments pour une théorie du système d'enseignement* (Paris: Minuit, 1970), p. 22.

12. Jean-Claude Milner, *De l'École* (Paris: Seuil, 1984), p. 14.

13. Lévi-Strauss, *Tristes Tropiques*, p. 186; p. 203.

14. Pierre Bourdieu, *Distinction: A Social Critique of the Judgment of Taste*, trans. R. Nice (Cambridge: Harvard University Press, 1984), p. 84; *La Distinction: Critique sociale du jugement* (Paris: Minuit 1979), p. 50.

15. Lévi-Strauss, *Structural Anthropology*, trans. C. Jacobson and B. G. Schoepf (New York: Basic Books, 1963), p. 21; *Anthropologie structurale*, 2 vols. (Paris: Plon, 1974), 1:28.

16. Michel Foucault, *The Order of Things* (New York: Vintage, 1973), p. 385; *Les Mots et les choses* (Paris: Gallimard, 1966), p. 397.

17. Foucault, "L'Homme est-il mort?" *Arts*, June 15, 1966, quoted in Luc Ferry, Alain Renaut, *La Pensée 68* (Paris: Gallimard, 1985), p. 41.

18. Edmund Leach, *Genesis as Myth and Other Essays* (London: Cape, 1969); *L'Unité de l'homme et autres essais*, trans. Guy Durand (Paris: Gallimard, 1980), p. 388.

19. Lévi-Struass, *Totemism*, trans. R. Needham (Boston: Beacon Press, 1963), p. 70; *Le Totémisme aujourd'hui* (Paris: P.U.F., 1962), p. 101.

20. Aimé Césaire, *Discourse on Colonialism*, trans. J. Pinkham (New York: Monthly Review Press, 1972), pp. 21–22; *Discours sur le colonialisme* (Paris: Présence africaine, 1955), pp. 19–20.

21. Ibid, p. 22; p. 20.

22. Hélé Béji, *Désenchantement national* (Paris: La Découverte, 1982), p. 118.

23. Frantz Fanon, *The Wretched of the Earth*, trans. C. Farrington, preface by J.-P. Sartre (New York: Grove, 1968), p. 47; *Les Damnés de la terre* (Paris: Maspéro, 1961), p. 33.

24. Ibid., p. 41; p. 31.

25. Ibid., p. 43; p. 34.

26. Ibid., p. 43; p. 33.

27. Karl Marx, "Drafts of an article on Friedrich List's book *Das Nationale System der politischen oekonomie*," in Marx and Engels, *Collected Works* (London: Lawrence and Wishart, 1975), 4:280; "A propos du Sys-

tème national de l'économie politique de Friedrich List," in *Oeuvres III* (Paris: Gallimard, coll. *La Pléiade*, 1982), 3:1435.

28. Joseph V. Stalin, "Marxism and the National Question" in *Selected Works* (Davis, Cal.: Cardinal, 1971), p. 53; *Le Communisme et la Russie* (Paris: Denöel, coll. Médiations, 1968), p. 85.

29. Marx and Engels, "The German Ideology," in Lewis S. Feuer, *Marx and Engels* (London: Fontana, 1972, p. 288; *L'Idéologie allemande*, in *Oeuvres III* (Paris: Gallimard, coll. *La Pléiade*, 1982), 3:1057.

30. Octavio Paz, *Rire et pénitence* (Paris: Gallimard, 1983), p. 85. Note that this citation is for a French collection of various essays by Paz. There is an English translation of the essay "Laughter and Penitence" in *Essays in Mexican Art* (New York: Harcourt, 1993). But this is not the source of the quotation used by AF.—Trans.

31. Quoted in Pascal Bruckner, *The Tears of the White Man* (New York: Collier Macmillan, 1983), p. 105.

32. Frantz Fanon, *The Wretched of the Earth*, p. 149; p. 119. AF's italics.

33. Joseph Görres, quoted in Jacques Droz, *Le Romantisme politique en Allemagne* (Paris: Armand Collin, 1963), p. 149.

34. On the two forms of racism, see, in addition to the inaugural article by Jeanne Hersh, "Sur la notion de race," *Diogène* (1967), no. 59; Pierre-André Taguieff, "Le Néoracisme différentialiste," *Langue et société* (December 1985), no. 34; Arthur Kriegel, *La Race perdue* (Paris: P.U.F., 1983).

35. Césaire, *Discourse on Colonialism*, p. 14; p. 12.

36. Fanon, p. 50; p. 35.

37. Quoted in Zeev Sternhell, *Maurice Barrès et le nationalisme français* (Brussels: Complexe, 1985), p. 268.

38. Barrès, quoted in Benda, *The Treason of the Intellectuals*, p. 64; p. 56.

39. Lévi-Strauss, "Race and Culture," *The View from Afar*, pp. 14–15; *Le Regard éloigné*, p. 36.

40. Ibid., p. xiv; p. 15.

41. "Cultural identity, they said, was at the core of individual and collective personality, the vital principle that underlay the most authen-

tic decisions, behaviour and actions." World Conference on Cultural Policies: Mexico City, 26 July to 6 August 1982, *Final Report* (Paris: UNESCO, 1982), p. 22.

42. Ibid., pp. 10–11.

43. Ibid., p. 8.

44. UNESCO, 4/9.3/2, "Declaration on Fundamental Principles Concerning the Contribution of the Mass Media to Strengthening Peace and International Understanding, to the Promotion of Human Rights and to countering Racialism, Apartheid and Incitement to War," *Records of the General Conference, 20th Session, Paris, 24 October to 28 November 1978, Resolutions* (Paris: UNESCO, 1979), pp. 102–3.

45. Ibid.

46. Lévi-Strauss, *The View From Afar*, p. xiv; *Le Regard éloigné,* p. 15.

47. Julien Benda, *La Fin de l'éternel* (Paris: Gallimard, 1977), p. 82.

48. Lévi-Strauss, *The View From Afar*, p. xiv; *Le Regard éloigné,* p. 15.

Part Three. Toward a Multicultural Society?

1. Robert Jaulin, quoted in Alain de Benoist, "Le Totalitarisme raciste," in *Eléments* (February-March 1980), no. 33, p. 15.

2. Michel Poniatowski, *Paris-Match*, November 8, 1985, p. 51.

3. To give an example from France, there was the attempt in 1986 to rewrite the nationality code. At first glance the spirit of the reform reflected the voluntary nature of citizenship and did not seem discrimatory. Had the law been passed, children born in France of foreign parents would have had to make a formal request to become French citizens between the ages of sixteen and twenty-three. Within that group the following could not apply: young people sentenced to prison terms for more than six months, or for any length of time, if the crime committed inflicted deliberate bodily harm or involved theft or the use or sale of drugs. Such undesirables were to be marked forever as delinquents and foreigners. Their wish to be citizens in no way changed the balance of

things: they had bad souls and could not, therefore, become French. Banished from the community of free men, they would receive Algerian passports whether they wanted them or not, which was, in effect, like giving them passports of an unwelcomed race of people. Under the pretext of preventing individuals from becoming French if they did not pursue their citizenship actively, this proposal reintroduced an essentialist interpretation of nationality, contrary to any philosophical commitment to choice. It used the elective theory of the nation as a cover for a legal maneuver whose ultimate goal was to *purify* the national community. Reviving fantasies of ethnic nationality, it linked the need to keep foreigners out with programs for eliminating Evil. For political reasons having little to do with my analysis here, the reform failed. What is important, however, in the context of this essay, is that a proposal such as this could have received serious attention by a government in a country like France.

4. Régis Debray, *La Puissance et les rêves* (Paris: Gallimard, 1984), pp. 183–84.

5. Ibid., p. 186.

6. Régis Debray, *Critique of Political Reason*, trans. D. Massey (London: Verso/New Left Books, 1983), p. 141; *Critique de la raison politique* (Paris: Gallimard, 1981), p. 206.

7. Montesquieu quoted in *Critique de la raison politique*, p. 331.

8. Ibid., p. 331.

9. Ibid.

10. Collège de France, *Propositions pour l'enseignment de l'avenir* (Paris: Collège de France, 1985).

11. Lévi-Strauss, *Entretiens avec Georges Charbonnier* (Paris: 10/18, 1961), p. 180.

12. Goethe, *Ecrits sur l'art* (Paris: Klincksieck, 1983), p. 50.

13. AF borrows this term from Milan Kundera, *The Art of the Novel*, trans. L. Asher (from the French) (New York: Grove Press, 1986), p. 44; *L'Art du roman* (Paris: Gallimard, 1986), p. 63—Trans.

14. AF borrows this expression from Leszek Kolakowski, "Les intel-

lectuels contra l'intellect," *L'Esprit révolutionnaire*, trans. J. Dewitte (Brussels: Complexe, 1978), p. 79—Trans.

15. Collège de France, *Propositions pour l'enseignement de l'avenir*, p. 12.

16. Kundera, "Un Occident kidnappé," *Le Débat* (November 1983), no. 27, p. 17.

17. Emmanuel Lévinas, *Difficult Freedom: Essays on Judaism*, trans. S. Hand (Baltimore: Johns Hopkins University Press, 1990), p. 178; *Difficile Liberté* (Paris, Albin Michel, 1976), p. 232.

18. Goethe, *Ecrits sur l'art*, p. 263.

19. Witold Gombrowicz, *Diary (1957–1961)*, trans. L. Vallee, 3 vols. (Evanston, Ill.: Northwestern University Press, 1989), 2:15. First published as *Dziennik 1957–61* (Paris: Instytut Lieracki, 1962).

20. Lévinas, "Portrait," in *Les Nouveaux Cahiers* (Fall 1985), no. 82, p. 34.

21. Marcel Gauchet, "Tocqueville, l'Amérique et nous," *Libre* (1980), no. 7, p. 95.

22. Ernst Bloch, *Droit naturel et dignité humaine* (Paris: Payot, 1976), p. 158.

23. Marx, "Contributions to the Critique of Hegel's *Philosophy of Right*," in R. Tucker, ed., *The Marx-Engels Reader*, trans. T. B. Bottomore (New York: Norton, 1972), p. 13; *Oeuvres III* (Paris: Gallimard, coll. La Pléiade, 1982), 3:384.

24. Father M. Lelong, quoted in Sadeck Sellam, "Etre musulman en France," *Etudes*, May 1986, p. 586.

25. Benda, *Discours à la nation européene* (Paris: Gallimard, coll. Idées, 1979), p. 71.

Part Four. We Are the World, We Are the Children

1. Gilles Deleuze and Félix Guattari, *Kafka: Toward a Minor Literature*, trans. D. Polan (Minneapolis: University of Minnesota Press, 1986), p. 18; *Kafka* (Paris: Minuit), 1975, p. 33. AF's italics.

2. Jacques Séguéla, in *Le Point*, February 24, 1986.

3. Yves Mourousi is a television journalist; Touré Kunda is a band from Senegal; Renaud and Bernard Lavilliers are French popular singers—Trans.

4. Harlem Désir, in *Espaces 89: L'Identité française* (Paris: Editions Tierce, 1985), p. 120. Harlem Désir was the president of the organization S.O.S. Racism, which was founded in 1984—Trans.

5. This kind of blackmail was in full swing during the big student demonstrations taking place in Paris in November 1986. When a newspaper editorial brazenly proclaimed that the students had been infected with "mental AIDS," Jack Lang, the former minister of cultural affairs, who was very popular with the students, retorted: "So here we have the culture of members of the Chirac-Hersant faction. Contempt for the young, hatred of music, of rock, of Coluche and Renaud." Are Coluche and Renaud part of the culture? Are music and rock the same? Is rock modern music or a return to a simpler form with a universal rhythm? From now on it is impossible to ask such questions, to criticize *at the same time* police violence and the blathering on of an ideologue. You now have to choose sides between rock and repression. The right to think independently used to protect one from fascist apologies for the use of brute force; today such autonomy is prohibited in the name of antifascism.

Coluche is a French music-hall performer—Trans.

6. André Bercoff, *Manuel d'instruction civique pour temps ingouvernables* (Paris: Grasset, 1985), p. 86ff.

7. Robert von Musil, *The Man Without Qualities*, trans. E. Wilkins and E. Kaiser, 3 vols. (London: Secker and Warburg, 1953), 1:46. Originally published as *Der Mann ohne Eigenschaften* (1930), vol. 1.

8. Guy Scarpetta, "Esquisses viennoises," in *Lettre internationale* (1986), no. 8, p. 59.

9. Martin Heidegger, "Overcoming Metaphysics," *The End of Philosophy*, trans. J. Stambaugh (New York: Harper and Row, 1973), p. 99 (originally *Vorträge und Aufsätze*, 1954).

10. Hannah Arendt, "The Crisis in Culture," in *Past and Future* (New York: Penguin, [1961] 1978), pp. 207–8; *La Crise de la culture* (Paris: Gallimard, coll. Idées, 1973), p. 266.

11. Octavio Paz, *Rire et pénitence* (Paris: Gallimard, 1983), p. 93. Note that this citation is for a French collection of various essays by Paz. There is an English translation of the essay "Laughter and Penitence" in *Essays in Mexican Art* (New York: Harcourt, 1993) But this is not the source of the quotation used by AF—Trans.

12. Marcel Gauchet, "Tocqueville, l'Amérique et nous," *Libre* (1980), no. 7, p. 71.

13. Condorcet, *Rapport et projet de décret pour l'organisation générale de l'Instruction publique*, avril 1792, quoted in Bronislaw Baczko, *Une Éducation pour la démocratie* (*Textes de l'époque révolutionnaire*) (Paris: Garnier, 1982).

14. Gilles Lipovetsky, *L'Ère du vide* (Paris: Gallimard, 1983), p. 183.

15. Ibid., p. 64.

16. Even if we remain on strictly political grounds, it is naive to feel happy about this world. Hanging loose, "cool," functionally allergic to all forms of totalitarianism, the postmodern subject is not willing or ready to fight against it when necessary. The defense of democracy does not mobilize him to action any more than a threat to his values does. It was, for example, enough for an imprisoned French terrorist merely to warn the jurors at his trial about the "harshness of proletarian justice" for the majority of them to call in sick, thereby interrupting the legal process. In other words, let us not rejoice too quickly: the other side of casual indifference to big causes is a willingness to abdicate in the face of force. As fanaticism disappears in Western societies, it may well be replaced by another kind of sickness of the spirit, hardly any less worrisome, namely, collaboration.

17. George Steiner, *In Bluebeard's Castle* (London: Faber and Faber, 1971), p. 66; *Dans le château de Barbe-Bleu (Notes pour une redéfinition de la culture)* (Paris, Gallimard, 1986), p. 95.

18. See Neil Postman, *Amusing Ourselves to Death* (New York: Viking, 1985), p. 94.

19. Hervé Hamon and Patrick Rotman, *Tant qu'il y aura des profs* (Paris: Seuil, 1984), p. 311.

20. Paul Yonnet, *Jeux, modes et masses* (Paris: Gallimard, 1985), pp. 185–86. AF's italics.

21. Stefan Zweig, *The World of Yesterday* (Lincoln: University of Nebraska Press, [1943] 1964), p. 34. The original German appeared after the English translation as *Die Welt von gestern. Erinnerunge eines Europaers* (Stockholm: Bermann-Fischer, 1946).

22. Federico Fellini, *Fellini on Fellini*, trans. from Italian and French by I. Quigley (New York: Delacorte Press, 1976). Originally published in German as *Aufsatze und Notizen* (Zurich: Diogenes Verlag, 1974); *Fellini par Fellini* (Paris: Calmann-Lévy, 1984), p. 163. Note that English edition does not contain the quotation cited here —Trans.

23. Philippe Gildas, *Télérama*, December 31, 1986, no. 1929.

24. Paul Yonnet, "L'Esthétique rock," *Le Débat* (1986), no. 40, p. 66.

25. Ibid., p. 71.

INDEX

Colonists, third world people as, 89

Communication, youth culture and, 134

Communism, decline of, 74-75

Community: God and, 17; humans and, 16; Renan's ideas of, 32; *see also* Cultural community

Comte, Auguste, 139*n*19

Condorcet, Marquis de, 52-53, 58, 126

Constitution: de Maistre's views, 14-15; revolutionary view, 13; U.S. minorities' challenges to, xvii

Consumerism, 125; and culture, 124-25; and education, 126-27

Contract-nation, French Enlightenment model, xiii

Cosmopolitanism, cultural identity and, 76

Counterrevolution, eighteenth-century, 19-20; and human nature, 25; and independent thought, 23-24; and transcendental values, 18

Creativity, postmodernism and, 114

Cultural community, 79; human rights and, xv; nation as, Stalin's idea, 73-74; racism and, 79

Cultural identity, 76-77, 79, 135; decolonization and, 67-69; education and, 82-83; and immigrants, 108; liberation movements and, 71-72, 74; multiculturalism and, 105; and Other, 89-90; politics of, 69-70; views of, 142*n*50, 145-46*n*41

Cultural imperialism, modern historians and, 58-59

Cultural relativism, xv, xvii-xviii, 94-100, 107; Lévi-Strauss and, xiv; and youth culture, xvi

Culture(s): adolescence of, 133-34; anthropology and, 57; calculative thinking and, 120-21; change in meaning of, 5-6; consumption and, 124-25; definitions, 1, 127; diversity of, 79; Enlightenment and, 123; equality of, 63-64; German, 9-10; and identity, 92; individual rights and, 106; language and, 129; multiculturalism and, 92; non-European, decolonization philosophy and, 67; plurality of, 59-61; postmodernism and, 112,